Trusted Voices

Trusted Voices

Spiritual Wisdom from
Lost Generations of Women

Diane Karay Tripp

Cover and interior design by Meredith Gruebbel

Published by Witherspoon Press, a ministry of the General
Assembly Council, Presbyterian Church (U.S.A.), 100 Witherspoon St.,
Louisville, Kentucky.

PRINTED IN THE UNITED STATES OF AMERICA
www.pcusa.org/witherspoon

ISBN 978-1571532039

Contents

The past interrupts the present
and is always the bearer of soul.

—Thomas Moore

Foreword

Once upon a time, in a faraway land, there lived a man. The man was blessed with three sons and seventeen camels. The man lived a contented life until he died.

Before he died, he bequeathed his precious camels to his beloved children in the following manner: To his firstborn, one-half of seventeen camels; to his second son, one-third; and to his youngest, one-ninth.

The father died. The three gathered to execute the father's bequest, but to their chagrin and great frustration, they realized that seventeen camels are not divisible by two—not without a big mess, at least. Furthermore, seventeen camels cannot be split equally into thirds or into ninths. Frustrated by their dilemma, the three children stared silently into one another's eyes.

Three days passed. Three days in which the siblings met regularly to discuss among themselves various dimensions of their shared conundrum, and yet to no avail. Once stumped, forever stumped.

On the third day, they noticed an approaching caravan. Wisdom approached, riding a camel. She disembarked and said, "Please add my camel to your lot, and try again."

The eldest exclaimed, "Eighteen camels can be divided in half—nine camels!"

The middle child discovered, "Eighteen camels can be split by three—six camels!"

And the youngest revealed, "Eighteen camels can be divided by nine—two camels! Nine camels plus six camels plus two camels equals seventeen camels."

With that, Wisdom climbed up on her camel and rode away.[1]

Trusted Voices

I love that story! It speaks about traditions passed from one generation to the next; about subsequent generations who are not quite sure what to do with the traditions they've been given; and about Wisdom, the gift from God that illumines the inheritance so that each generation might find strength, comfort, and guidance for living within it.

Diane Karay Tripp shines a light on the Reformed stream of the Christian tradition that draws significant voices from the shadows of history, trusted voices of wise women who have proclaimed the grace and gifts of God. And what do we do with this inheritance, these voices long forgotten? Listen to them!

Karay Tripp's gift to Christ's beloved community redounds with spiritual insight regarding women and spirituality. She entwines their personal stories with wisdom she has received from them, modeling a receptive faith that intends to listen before it speaks. Unfortunately, the silence that listening requires can be incorrectly perceived as muted docility, as if women have nothing to say or add to the conversation of faith. Quite the contrary. Women of the Reformed faith have had plenty to say, but their voices have been silenced and their faithful witness has been relegated to the sidelines of history by those who have deemed their contributions to be of little value. With that assertion comes a point of inestimable value: power structures that consider women to be subordinate members of society maintain a false equilibrium by silencing them. This false balance shapes their experiences in ways that protect the advantage of the powerful. Unlocking these voices may lead the reader to wonder about unlocking other things, not the least of which is a spiritual tradition that has almost exclusively remembered the experiences of men to its own detriment.

So consider this book the eighteenth camel so generously offered by a wise woman. Sit with it, listen, and reflect on its treasures. Choose one or more of these women as a spiritual guide for your personal journey. Reflect on the words, let them resound through your soul so that you may find your own voice. May those who come after us find our voices trustworthy.

—Mark Hinds, Editor

---

1. Mark Hinds, "Wisdom's Gift: Generation X and the Problem of Print-Oriented Religious Education," *Religious Education* 96, no. 4 (Fall 2001): 511–12.

Introduction

I was a five-year-old "feminist" in 1960. At kindergarten recess, boys refused to let girls near playground equipment. Day after day I watched the boys run and listened to their taunts while the teacher looked away. I simmered at the injustice. One day I exploded and ran for the swings as the boys chased me. I fell, scraping a knee. Despite pain, I settled into a swing and flew high in defiance.

My freedom run attracted no imitators, and it was hard to sustain my native feminism in isolation. This was the early 1960s. We learned to read from Dick and Jane books. Many women went on errands sporting plastic curlers on their heads. The image of the housewife at leisure eating bonbons was a common cliché. Lucy Ricardo whined and got into mischief. My respect for women eroded.

Men ushered us into the sanctuary, preached, blessed and distributed communion. One year a female elder joined the males in performing a solemn walk between chancel and sanctuary, carrying communion plates and cups. Her presence was a declaration I could not understand.

On Sunday mornings I searched the church's magnificent stained glass window. Christ crucified and risen dominated the window. Male apostles flanked him and surrounded the first communion table. I found only two women: Eve, expelled from Paradise by an angel throwing a thunderbolt, and the Virgin Mary, nestled beside Jesus' manger. Much later, close inspection revealed girls waiting to be blessed by Jesus and three women keeping vigil at the cross. I have no memories of women mentioned in sermons. Girls and women infiltrated the chancel by singing in choirs and playing the organ.

One summer I surveyed the sky for enemy bombers. I worked on 4-H projects at the sewing machine and listened to the Beatles on the radio. In November 1963, an otherwise unmemorable Girl Scout meeting was seared into memory with the announcement that President Kennedy had been shot. Starlets were spoken of in subdued tones and deemed unsuitable role models. We watched Mighty Mouse, Captain Kangaroo, Lassie reruns, and Ed Sullivan. My sister collected Beatles and Elton John albums while I perched in a wild cherry tree and pretended to be an Indian at one with nature. The church hired a female assistant minister. She had been a scientist but had no talent for preaching. I was disappointed and did not miss her when she left.

I had no one to look up to. I took my mother for granted and did not learn any lessons from her managerial skills in raising four daughters and seeing them off to college. Our family doctor was male. The pastor from whom I learned how to preach was a man. So was the president. I did not know of any women reporters, zookeepers, or paleontologists, professions that appealed to me for brief periods of time. I was not invited to spend a day with my father at work. Children scarcely qualified as "people," and girls were less people than others.

I was deprived of role models who were taken for granted by previous generations of women. I had no idea that Protestants used to read spiritual memoirs by women. I did not know that women had served as spiritual guides and changed lives and neighborhoods. I was unaware that the Reformed tradition had its mystics and that early American Indian women had watched over the souls of new converts; unaware that I might yet find warm, compassionate, and wise women from the past who embodied all that any woman might aspire to be.

We needed to know that history was not the sole province of men with crowns, guns, treaties, and constitutions. We needed to know that church history included women. Roman Catholics revered martyrs, saints, and the Blessed Virgin Mary. Reformed women, it seemed to me, looked to men with a vague sense of being relegated to the sidelines.

Previous generations discarded the records of women's voices. We never knew what we were missing until Betty Friedan suggested that the loss was substantial. We discovered how thoroughly we had been excluded, how many barriers were set against us, how the pain of exclusion and prejudice was multiplied in the lives of countless women. As we marched, held sit-ins, and met together, unease gave way to awareness, one person at a time, as if we were awakening from a bad dream. We sensed new possibilities and asked: "Who can I trust? Am I alone?"

Introduction

Walter Brueggemann wrote that when faced with temptation, Jesus was not alone in the wilderness, but, having in his heart Hebrew Scriptures and "faith memories," was "in the company of many ancient, faithful, trusted voices that told him who he was."[1] Our foremothers had many voices they trusted to impart wisdom and to give encouragement. Our generation never heard them. It was as if notable women ceased to exist after the Reformation. We had looked to ancient and medieval women for wisdom, unaware of Reformed female mystics and guides.[2]

I discovered Isabella Graham's memoir in an Oxford bookstore in 1990 when my late husband, David, and I lived in England. The din of a jackhammer almost sent me fleeing. But I had a sense I should stay put and came across an 1816 first edition of her book. I found other accounts of women on microfilm and gradually came to realize that they were an astounding group of spiritual leaders and models of strength and wisdom never met in church school, college, seminary, or bookstores. I wondered why they had been excised from our collective memory.

We need their stories to understand who we are. We need their voices to help us discover who we might become. We need models of women who love God, venerable ancestors to inspire us.

This volume seeks to give you access to the spiritual experience and counsel of women whose narratives are long out of print, whose wisdom has been silenced by neglect—women from lost generations. Listen to them with your heart. You are in the company of many faithful, trusted voices who will help you discover your identity as child of God.

Here you will meet twenty-five American and British women, mostly spiritual guides, mystics, and spiritual exemplars who lived from the early 1600s into the late 1800s. Four were Native American and two, African American. All were Reformed: Presbyterian or Congregational. Their wisdom has universal resonance. The writings of contemporary women are not included since they are widely available.

The subjects were conscious of being women before God and of reading Scripture through women's eyes. The Scottish Presbyterian mystic Marion Laird pondered, "Where in all of Scripture is it said, 'Let a woman ask wisdom of God'?" Bestselling author Dorothy Leigh identified with the nursing mother in Isaiah (*49:15*) as well as with Paul's childbirth imagery (*Gal. 4:19*). Sarah Davy took heart from the woman healed after touching the hem of Christ's garment

Trusted Voices

(*Luke 8:43–48*). Mystic Elisabeth West seized on the harlot of Ezekiel 16 as an appropriate metaphor for her sinfulness. Elizabeth Cairns learned that Christ is like a woman who carries an infant yet makes a toddler walk alone and deals with souls in like fashion. Susanna Anthony was painfully aware that she could not minister publicly in the sanctuary, so she consecrated herself to God's "public service in a private, secret way." Hannah Sinclair urged her readers to be like the importunate widow, relentless in the pursuit of blessing. Across the generations, women favored a verse from Proverbs: "[Wisdom's] ways are ways of pleasantness, and all her paths are peace" (*3:17*).

They inherited a tradition of receiving guidance from other women, which probably predates the Reformation and may have roots in ancient Celtic practice. The Englishwoman Briget Cooke, who died in the late 1630s, was a discerning physician of the soul trusted by others. She herself took spiritual guidance from an older woman whom she called "Mother," in recognition of her eminence in grace. Generation after generation maintained a chain of spiritual companionship through personal acquaintance, word of mouth, and reading.

A large proportion of the women portrayed here were spiritual directors or guides to others. These include the former slave Catherine Ferguson and the Native American Abiah Paaonit. Others were Elizabeth Bury, Catharine Dimmick, Isabella Graham, Marion Laird, Dorothy Leigh, Elizabeth Prentiss, Sarah Osborn, Mary Simpson, Hannah Sinclair, and Fanny Woodbury. Leigh and Sinclair exercised guidance primarily through writing; the others, through personal interaction, counseling, and letters.

Several were sought out by ministers, foreigners, and complete strangers. Large numbers visited Marion Laird. Elizabeth Bury, Catharine Dimmick, and Elizabeth Prentiss were married to pastors and had the enthusiastic support of their husbands. Bury, Dimmick, Ferguson, Graham, Osborn, and Mary Rich were highly respected for their ministry among the poor and oppressed. Osborn, furthermore, began antislavery efforts in her area by educating and mentoring African Americans.

The next largest category of women included spiritual exemplars who were an inspiration to their families and a smaller circle of people. Abigail Ammapoo, a nearly blind religious teacher and perhaps a deacon, dedicated her life to serving God through serving others. Young Jerusha Ohquanhut was known for her faithful prayer after a privateer abducted her father. Prayer permeated Mary Hutson's

Introduction

life and she endeavored to embody the Christ-centeredness that she sought to nurture in her children. Elizabeth Moore won the admiration of an eminent minister. Sarah Davy left behind a volume titled *Record of my Consolations and the Meditations of my Heart* that breathes a tender spirituality. Countess Mary Rich, who once ignored ministers, was transformed into a very devout person and ministered to others through expansive charity, herbal medicine, and a letter of spiritual guidance, "Rules for a Holy Life." Susanna Anthony was an invalid known for her gift of prayer and had a soul-friendship with the dynamo Sarah Osborn.

Four Scottish women were mystics: Elizabeth Cairns, Marion Laird, Mary Somervel, and Elisabeth West. West's memoir was popular and "stood as a standard of evangelical Presbyterian devotion,"[3] while Marion Laird's astounding memoir has been neglected for centuries. God touched Elizabeth Cairns when she was a child shepherd. After being orphaned at the age of ten, Mary Somervel felt so consoled by divine love that she was lost in ecstasy. Elisabeth West was bitten hard by a dog at church, presaging hard trials in which she fought to keep awake to pray and warred with unbelief. Marion Laird's spiritual narrative and letters of guidance are, to my knowledge, the richest testament bequeathed us by a Reformed woman writing in English.

Finally, we have three conversion accounts. New England slave Phillis Cogswell's conversion narrative was recorded when she sought church membership. Temperance Hannibal, a Montaukett Native American from Long Island, New York, leaves the briefest of historical footprints, just two paragraphs about her spiritual awakening. Deborah Prince probably feasted on conversations between her father and evangelist George Whitefield and theologian Jonathan Edwards. After a model pious girlhood she was afflicted by fears that she was just another hell-bound sinner. Her (re)conversion took place, proverbially, on her deathbed. Her story is included as a reminder that religion is interwoven with our emotional and bodily health and that we can all benefit from the discernment of impartial soul friends.

God is the central actor in this book. With their consent, God re-created these women as witnesses to love. Don't assume that because their stories have been submerged in old books they have nothing new to say. God uses the cloud of witnesses to energize and teach us. In the words of John Calvin, "The virtues of the saints are testimonies that strengthen us, so that depending on them as our companions, we may come to God more swiftly."[4]

Reflection Questions

Do you have an early memory that remains vivid? What does this memory tell you about yourself? About your culture?

As a young person, did you have any role models? A spiritual mentor? If so, can you sum up what wisdom that person gave you? If not, explore what anchored you.

Who is your "trusted voice" now? Who energizes your soul?

Do you have a favorite spiritual book? Recall or share why it speaks to you. Have several friends from different parts of your life been recommending the same book to you? This may be the Spirit's way of suggesting further reading.

Notes

1. *Inscribing the Text: Sermons and Prayers of Walter Brueggemann* (Minneapolis: Fortress Press, 2004), p. 38.
2. Even now as academic writers produce articles and books chronicling the lives, leadership, and theology of Reformed women, among others, little or no attempt has been made to provide laypeople access to their spiritual writing. See, for example: Elizabeth A. Clark and Herbert Richardson, eds., *Women and Religion: The Original Sourcebook of Women in Christian Thought*, new rev. and expanded ed. (San Francisco: HarperSanFrancisco, 1996); Susan Hill Lindley, *"You Have Stept Out of your Place": A History of Women and Religion in America* (Louisville, KY: Westminster John Knox Press, 1996); Eleanor J. Stebner, *The Women of Hull House: A Study in Spirituality, Vocation, and Friendship* (Albany: State University of New York Press, 1997).
3. Leigh Eric Schmidt, *Holy Fairs: Scottish Communions and American Revivals in the Early Modern Period* (Princeton: Princeton University Press, 1989), p. 47.
4. Latin epilogue on the title page of Hugh Bryan and Mary Hutson, *Living Christianity Delineated* (London, 1760). From *Epist. Ad Heb.* Cap. xii, Ver. 1. Trans. by D. H. Tripp.

I

Dorothy Leigh, d. 1616

I Labor That Christ May Be Formed in You

The excuse most people offer the hosts of television's "What Not to Wear" when indicted for fashion crimes is "But it's comfortable!" We are experts at comfortable clothing, comfortable surroundings, and "comfort food," yet comfort of heart can be elusive. We don't need national exposure in prime time to know we need help refashioning our soul. We need gentle advice from a soul friend. Consider one such woman and her good counsel.

In Stuart England, women were expected to be silent, pious, and self-effacing. Empowered by her roles as a Puritan wife and mother, Dorothy Leigh became an outspoken spiritual leader to a wide audience with the publication of her book *The Mothers Blessing* (1616), perhaps the best-selling women's book of the seventeenth century.[1] (Puritans were those who wanted to purify the church from within, simplify worship, be diligent in personal and family devotions, and lead a worthy Christian life.)

Dorothy was born into a prosperous family, one of four children of Elizabeth Higham and Robert Kempe. She married Ralph Leigh, about whom little is known, and bore three sons, George, John, and William. When Ralph died, he left a will directing Dorothy to secure their children's education.

Having a sense that her life was drawing to a close, Dorothy realized she could fulfill this parental duty by leaving a book of instruction. Presuming that a manuscript left with the eldest son was unlikely to reach the youngest and desiring to reach a wider audience, she wrote for publication.

Dorothy was aware that she would be criticized for publishing her views but defended herself: "Could Saint Paul wish himself separated from God for his brethren's sake and will not a mother venture to offend the world for her children's sake? Therefore let no man blame a mother, though she something exceed in writing to her children. . . ."[2]

She, like God, would not forget her children: "Can a woman forget her nursing child or show no compassion for the child of her womb? Even these may forget, yet I will not forget you." "My mind will continue long after me in writing," she assured them.[3] Again she refers to Saint Paul:

"My little children, for whom I am again in the pain of childbirth until Christ is formed in you, I wish I were present with you now. . . ." "Is it possible," Dorothy asked, "that she which hath carried her child within her, so near her heart, and brought it forth into this world with so much bitter pain, so many groans and cries, can forget it? Nay, rather, will she not labor now till Christ be formed in it?"[4]

Dorothy Leigh accepted the call to spiritual motherhood—guiding souls to birth in Christ—and her labor bore fruit for countless other Christians. Do we nurture and strengthen others as they seek God or do we hinder them on their pilgrimage? Every day brings us a new opportunity to help others.

Read these passages from Dorothy Leigh's best-selling *The Mothers Blessing* and discover why many people cherished her counsel. She assures us that the Holy Spirit expects our prayers, discloses why examining our consciences and confessing our sin to God are important, and reveals the source of all contentment and peace of heart.

The Spirit of God Is Calling Thee
"Never make account of thyself as a diligent servant of God, if thou dost not twice a day (at the least) come privately to God and acknowledge thy infirmities and confess that thou canst not pray, and desire God to give thee grace to do it faithfully. When thou feelest a motion to pray, do not overslip it for any cause in the world, for thou knowest not what graces or blessings God means to bestow upon thee at that time, for it is the Spirit of God calling thee. Therefore find no delays, but go."[5]

Rooting Out Weeds
"I desire you, and every one of yours to the world's end, that whatsoever service of God you omit, you do not neglect private prayer; for many may hear the word of God, as Adam did, and disobey it presently after; and some hear the word of God as Adam did after his fall, and had rather be further off, as he had then. But

private prayer is to offer thyself and thy service to God, confessing thy own imperfections, and to call to God for his assistance.

"Now when a sinner by himself calleth his own ways to remembrance and confesseth his particular sins, then he seeth what sin his own nature is most subject to, and prayeth earnestly against that sin wherewith he is most infected, and confesseth his own weakness and wondereth at himself that he is not able to overcome that one sin as well as some other sins of as great force. The reason is this: the nature of man is wholly corrupted with sin and is good for nothing, as the earth is fit to bring forth nothing but weeds except it be digged and dressed and continually labored and weeded: yet one weed or other will grow in some part of the earth by nature which will not grow in another part though it be sown there, but some other weed will grow there that is as ill, and one weed overgrowing the ground is able to make it unprofitable for anything.

"So one sin will rule where another will not, and that one overrunning thee is able to make thee an unprofitable member of the church. Therefore thou must labor by private prayer to overcome it."[6]

Peace of Heart
"To lay hold of Christ is the best thing in the world. It is the most pleasing thing because it brings so sweet contentment to the soul, mind, and conscience of man, that nothing can offend it. It is the most comfortable thing in [that] it so comforteth and strengtheneth the heart, that nothing can grieve it. It is most profitable, for it getteth an everlasting kingdom to those that use it. It is most delightful, for it bringeth joy to the whole man. It is most contenting, for no cross in the world can discontent it; when as the world on the contrary side are never content, never quiet, never feel joy in their hearts. Though they laugh, their hearts are not quiet, for 'there is no peace to the ungodly' (Isaiah 48:22).

"And this is the cause that they seek so much for pastime and sit up in the night swilling and drinking until they feel sleep call them to bed, and they lie down like brute beasts, never regarding the misspending of their time nor calling for grace to spend the rest of their days better.

"And yet, for all this, in the dark they often feel discontent in their minds because they do follow the devil, that wicked serpent, which will torment them. And he begins to torment them and yet they will serve him.

"On the contrary, those that serve God and follow Christ and every night reconcile themselves unto him and confess their own weakness and pray Christ their Savior to defend them that night and evermore, they feel much comfort in their hearts, for Christ begins the comfort here. 'I lay me down in peace and rose again,' saith David, 'and the Lord sustained me' (Psalm 3:5). So they which serve God and follow Christ are in peace, for the Lord sustaineth them."[7]

Reflection Questions

In what ways can you spiritually nurture others? Jesus helped those whom others didn't expect him to care about and he did so in unexpected ways. Think of creative ways to love, serve, and pray for others.

Gently examine your interactions with others, especially those with whom you are in conflict. How might your actions, words, and expectations affect them?

What words of spiritual counsel would you like to leave as a legacy to a young person? Perhaps you could make this the focus of a writing or craft project.

Are you a good spiritual role model? How can you improve? Pray for the grace to grow as you would like yourself to be.

Remember or describe a moment in which you felt God calling you to pray. How could you become more attentive to the promptings of the Spirit? Consider posting notes to yourself to remind yourself to pray in different settings: for example, you could leave notes in your walking/running shoes, in your car, on the bathroom mirror, or on a garden trowel or other tool.

Notes

1. Dorothy Leigh, *The Mothers Blessing* (London, 1616); Sylvia Brown, ed., *Women's Writing in Stuart England: The Mothers' Legacies of Dorothy Leigh, Elizabeth Joscelin, and Elizabeth Richardson* (Stroud: Sutton Publishing, 1999), p. 3.
2. Leigh, *The Mothers Blessing*, pp. 11–12. See Romans 9:3.
3. Ibid., pp. 9, 12; cf. Isaiah 49:15.
4. Galatians 4:19–20a; Leigh, *The Mothers Blessing*, pp. 9–10.
5. Leigh, *The Mothers Blessing*, pp. 72–73.
6. Ibid., pp. 79–81.
7. Ibid., pp. 87–89.

II

Mary Simpson, c. 1617–1647

I Gave Her Leave to Be the Preacher

Organ recitals are frowned on in my family. We all appreciate music and have musical abilities, but lengthy monologues on health matters are often dismissed as "organ recitals."

Some people allow discomfort and disease to consume all their attention. Others look beyond them. Here is the story of one person who was bedfast yet focused all her energy on helping others.

When pastor John Collings arrived in Norwich, England, he discovered a former maid in his new congregation who listened to parishioners' spiritual concerns. Mary Simpson was a Presbyterian Puritan within the Church of England whose first spiritual struggle concerned her perception that she neglected the day of rest. She became ill while still young and was confined to bed for the last three years of her life. Collings recalled her first words to him: "Sir, I beseech you tell me how I may glorify God in my affliction." She didn't dwell on her pain. "God had subdued her spirit to the feet of his own will," John observed.[1] Mary made peace with suffering and had a burning desire to praise God and to be an instrument of grace to others.

Although Mary could not leave her bedroom, visitors found their way to her. "I was taken up much . . . in the work of exhortation of friends that came to visit me," she wrote.[2] The young pastor described Mary's chamber as a "room of paradise," where all who entered "went away instructed, or satisfied, or quickened, or some way or other bettered."[3]

Nearly four centuries later, we can take heart from one pastor's witness to the counsel of a gifted woman:

"The greatest part of her work was angelical, a speaking well of God, admiring and exalting his free grace, telling what he had done for her soul. Yet she remembered that while she was in the body, she had a duty to do to others, and never did any labor more for God with the souls of others than this precious one. Grace had made her eloquent; her birth and breeding was mean, but the Lord had given her the tongue of the excellent. O the abundance of grace that was poured out into her lips!

"I appeal to you, did not your hearts burn within you when you heard her speak, the excellency of sense, spiritual sense? I sometimes (as my occasions permitted) went to visit her, and while I thought to speak, my ears silenced my tongue, and *gave her leave to be the preacher,* for the gain of those in the room and that I myself might learn righteousness. Whoever heard her mentioning her affliction? Discoursing of any worldly thing? O that my tongue were so sanctified!"[4]

Mary stressed the importance of prayer and urged people to seek deeper communion with God.

John Collings wished he could have spent more time listening to her instruction. He considered the times he had to be elsewhere "enemies to my happiness."[5]

Mary Simpson lived a short, simple, and hidden life but preached eloquent spiritual sense and brought people closer to God in a sickroom that blossomed like paradise. Perhaps she can teach us to be spiritually confident. Mary taught from a position of spiritual strength, and a young male minister fell quiet in order to listen to her wisdom. What is possible for us if we rest our faith in God?

In the following excerpts from her writing, Mary Simpson passes on wisdom gained in prayer: Christ's intercession supports and perfects our prayers; those who endure weary times of God's seeming absence are progressing into "faith beyond sight."

Christ's Intercession
"I found the actings of God in me and toward me. I prayed in another manner than before, that when I asked anything for myself or others, agreeable to God's will, especially in straits, I found a holy boldness and confidence that God would answer, and he did answer abundantly beyond what I can express, not because of my request, but because Jesus Christ interceded. He took my broken and imperfect requests and shattered expressions, and presented them blameless before

God; not because I prayed, but because he delighted to show mercy; and so engaged and encouraged me to wait upon him, in his service."[6]

Faith Beyond Sight

"The next thing I saw was that there was a faith which was according to sight, like that of Thomas: he believed because he saw; and another faith beyond sight, which was to believe upon the sight of the actings of grace plentifully upon my soul. When God withdrew the sense of his love so that I did not enjoy the daily incomes of God's love, I was constrained to live upon the immutability and unchangeableness of God.

"Notwithstanding the great mercy and favor of God formerly conveyed, I was constrained with David to cry out, 'Restore to me the joy of thy salvation.' And then I apprehended that Christ was absent, at which time I lived solitary and in the dark. I looked upon Christ as a husband, but yet as a husband going [on] a journey, and hid behind a curtain, so that my soul was as the spouse restless in looking out to inquire after him. But in time he sent many love letters to me which were these: 'To you that fear my name shall the Sun of righteousness arise with healing in his wings.' Though I did not fear him perfectly and as I ought, yet I had some desires to serve him in truth. And another was, 'He that shall come, will come, and will not stay.' Yet sometime by reason of his absence, I wondered what my temper was and said, 'What is God about to teach me? Oh, that I knew his mind! And I would do it. Oh, that I knew what my present condition were!' And in time God graciously came in with this Scripture and persuaded me with Paul, that the life I now lived was by the faith of the Son of God, who loved me and gave himself for me; and that his grace was sufficient for me. And at last I saw him (behind the curtains). I saw him but could not enjoy him. At last I found him whom my soul loved."[7]

Reflection Questions

Sometimes sickness or suffering is an occasion for growing in spiritual wisdom. What have you learned during such times?

Would you have been open to this insight when healthy and content?

Express in your own words the Christian's grounds for "holy boldness." Can you think of a scriptural example?

Sometimes we painfully feel the absence of God. Jesus said, "It is to your advantage that I go away . . ." (*John 16:7*). What advantage does God give us in times of spiritual dryness?

Mary Simpson felt that God sent her "love letters" in the form of Scripture verses. What scriptural encouragement has God highlighted for you? Have you written it down to bring it to mind more often?

Notes

1. John Collings, *Faith & Experience: Or, a Short Narration of the Holy Life and Death of Mary Simpson . . .*, in John Collings, *The Life and Death of a True Christian* (London, 1649).
2. Mary Simpson, *Confession of her faith and relation of her experience, taken from her owne mouth . . .*, in Collings, *Faith & Experience*, p. 47.
3. Ibid., p. 71.
4. Ibid., pp 71–73. Italics added by author.
5. Ibid., p. 68.
6. Simpson, *Confession*, pp. 32–33.
7. Ibid., pp. 42–45.

III

Elizabeth Moore, d. 1656?

This Day Thou Shalt Be with Me in Paradise

One of my mother's prayers is "Clear the dust from my eyes." As children we need to be taught to distinguish make-believe from truth. In spiritual life, too, we begin as children in need of teachers to help us become discerning. The Holy Spirit is our primary teacher. One woman who allowed the Spirit to cleanse her sight was Elizabeth Moore of London.

She was a poor Puritan who contracted breast cancer in midlife and died a year or two later. We don't know when she was born or how she learned to read and write well. Edmund Calamy I (1600–1666), the Presbyterian minister who was probably her pastor and published her *Evidences for Heaven,* gives us a glimpse into her spirituality.

When Edmund Calamy preached her funeral sermon in St. Mary Aldermanbury parish church, he recalled that during her illness, Elizabeth had many generous and compassionate friends through whom she felt God's love. He also observed that she bore pain with a sweet spirit and patience.

For many years, Elizabeth doubted her salvation and sought assurance. When she fell ill, her doubts disappeared and she enjoyed peaceful communion with God. Edmund recalled that she derived comfort and strength from Scripture. Two of her favorite chapters were Hebrews 12 and Romans 8. She also drew strength from 2 Corinthians 4:16: "So we do not lose heart. Even though our outer nature is wasting away, our inner nature is being renewed day by day."

The day Elizabeth died, her pastor recorded what happened. She woke from sleep radiant with joy and told those by her bedside that as she slept she heard a voice say, "This day thou shalt be with me in Paradise."[1]

Trusted Voices

Edmund, a distinguished minister, normally found dreams insufficient evidence of grace. But when he heard of Elizabeth's dream, he reasoned, "When a woman who hath spent many years in the service of God, and is visited by God for above a year, with great and most grievous pains, shall at the close of her life, have such a sweet, refreshing, and heart-cheering impression upon her spirit when heart fails and flesh fails, [and] when she can hardly speak to express the greatness of her joy, then to hear a voice saying, 'This day thou shalt be with me in Paradise,' this (in all probability) was the voice of God and not of man. This was the Lord's doing and it is marvelous in our eyes. . . .

"I forbear saying any more. She is gone from a prison to a palace, from a purgatory to a paradise. She is at rest with God where all tears are wiped away from her eyes. The Lord fit us by his grace to follow her in due time into the kingdom of glory. Amen."[2]

God graced Elizabeth with a sweet spirit in the midst of much pain. She drew close to God through Scripture and allowed its comfort to permeate her soul. May we hold on to God in times of pain or difficulty, praying that our inner nature may be renewed day by day. May we also be compassionate friends to those whom others pass by, the sick and the dying, all who mourn, languish in prison, and suffer otherwise. Christ gazes at us from the depths of their eyes.

In the following passages from *Evidences for Heaven*, Elizabeth Moore discloses how her eyes were opened and she found anchorage in Christ. She also shows us how this leads to a joyful perception of divine love in others.

A Hope That I Am Born from Above
"Now then, to prove whether I be indeed and in truth born again is my desire at this time. The Lord help me and give me a sincere and upright heart and guide me herein by his Holy Spirit for the honour of his holy Name.

"Blessed be God, who hath through his free mercy begotten me to a hope that I am regenerated and born from above and converted unto God.

"Reason, because the Lord hath gone the same usual way with me as with those he pleaseth to convert to himself, and this I shall make to appear in five or six particulars.

"1. The Lord by his Spirit accompanying the preaching of his Word, caused the scales to fall from my eyes and opened them and set up a clear light in my understanding, and made me to see sin, to be exceeding sinful, out of measure sinful, and to look on it as the loathsomest thing in the world, and on myself as a loathsome creature in God's sight and in my own sight, by reason of the leprosy of sin wherewith I was overrun.

2. The Lord brought me to see the misery that I was in by reason of my sins. I thought I was utterly forsaken of God, and I thought that God would never accept of such a wretch as I saw myself to be. I could not think otherwise but that hell was my portion, and that I, by reason of my sins, must go thither, expecting every day when the Lord would glorify himself in my damnation. I saw myself in more misery because of my sins than I could then or now express to anybody. I looked upon God as a consuming fire and on myself as stubble, ready to be consumed by him, etc.

3. The Lord brought me to a spiritual astonishment, that I cried out, 'What shall I do to be saved!' and said with Paul, 'Lord! What wouldest thou have me to do?' Do but make known to thy poor creature what thy will is, and I thought I could do anything or suffer anything for the Lord. But since I have had some more knowledge of the holy will of God, woe is me! What a barren and unfruitful heart have I! A heart that can neither do nor suffer anything for the Lord as I ought to do. But this I can say, that the astonishment I was in, by the sight of my sins and the misery I was plunged into, put me on the performance of holy duties, especially prayer.

4. The Lord took me off my own bottom, off my own righteousness, and made me to see that was but a sandy foundation and would not hold out. I was not taken off from the performance of holy duties; no, I thought with myself that I am commanded by God to perform holy duties, which is the way and means whereby we may meet with God (for he is ordinarily to be enjoyed nowhere but in his own ordinances), but the Lord took me off from resting and trusting in ordinances. And as he made me to see that without the practice of them he would not accept of me, so also he made me to know that it was not for holy duties for which I was accepted. The sins that cleave to my best performances are enough for which the Lord may justly condemn me, if I had no other sins.

5. The Lord brought me to see a superlative beauty and excellency in the Lord Jesus Christ, and my soul was deeply in love with him, even with [the] whole Christ in all his offices, and (if I know anything at all of my own heart) I desired Christ as much to be my king and prophet, to teach and guide me, and subdue me to himself and rule over me, as to be my high priest, to make atonement by offering up of himself for me and washing me in his blood, by which I must be justified.

6. The Lord brought me to see a soul satisfaction in the Lord Jesus Christ alone, and I think I should be as fully satisfied with Christ alone as my heart can desire. If I know my heart, it panteth after Christ and Christ alone: *None but Christ, none but Christ.* The whole world in comparison or competition with Christ is nothing to me. But in him I see full contentment. To see and know my interest in him and to enjoy communion with him is that which if the Lord would bestow upon me, I should with Jacob say, 'It is enough,' and with old Simeon, 'Now let thy servant depart in peace, for my eyes have seen thy salvation.' "[3]

My Delight Is in the Saints

"I find my heart much enflamed with love to all the children of God because they are God's children, and the more I see or find or hear of God in them, the more I find my heart cleaving to them, and I think I can truly say with David, that my delight is in the saints and those that excel in grace; not because they are friends to me or I have relation to them in regard of outward obligations, but because they bear the image of God upon them and manifest it in their holy conversation. I love them, whether rich or poor. And though I did never know some of them but only hear of their holiness and piety, yet I could not but exceedingly love such. Therefore I hope that I am passed from death to life because I love the brethren, 1 John 3:14."[4]

This Day Thou Shalt Be with Me in Paradise

Reflection Questions

In Scripture, Joseph, son of Jacob; Joseph, husband of Mary; and the Magi had dreams that brought messages of grace. Do you recall a dream that had a spiritual message? What supports the idea that your dream was inspired by the Holy Spirit?

Remember a spiritual turning point in your life. Pray for the grace to be open to continual formation in Christ.

Think of a person you know who embodies God's love. How do you feel when you are with this person? Perhaps that person sees God's image in you. What difference does this make to human interaction?

As you pass by people on the streets, be mindful if you are forming judgments of their character based on their appearance. Remind yourself they are made in God's image.

Notes

1. Edmund Calamy, *The Godly Mans Ark . . . Sermons, The first of which was Preached at the Funerall of Mistresse Elizabeth Moore . . . Hereunto are annexed Mris. Moores Evidences for Heaven . . .*, 2nd ed. (London, 1658), p. 230. The book was published by Moore's brother, John Hancock.
2. Ibid., pp. 231–32.
3. Ibid., pp. 236–241.
4. Ibid., p. 247.

IV

Sarah Davy, c. 1638–c. 1669

One Touch of Christ's Garment

An African minister friend told me that her people often face spiritual difficulty when they immigrate to the United States. "Is prayer difficult?" I asked. "To say the least of it," she replied. We live in a complex culture in which devotion to God is undermined by many voices competing for our attention. We are easily distracted, resist God, and often despair before we contemplate surrender to the One for whom nothing is impossible. The story of a soul friend may encourage you to make God your first—your natural—refuge.

Sarah Roane was born in England around 1638 to parents who taught her to pray and took her to church. She studied the catechism and claimed the Ten Commandments as her personal rule for living. When she was ten years old her mother died and soon after, she lost her brother. She said to herself, "The Lord made me, and he made me to serve him."[1] She felt the presence of the Holy Spirit and knew that God was watching over her. A year later she was indifferent to God.

By the time she finished boarding school and returned home, her church had a new minister. Sarah was deeply moved by his first sermon yet troubled by doubts and fears. Unable to reconcile doubt and faith, she concluded she was a hypocrite and prayed for help, a prayer soon answered when her family moved to a new home. Here she found spiritual support in the friendship of a devout Congregationalist woman and her church family and joined the church through admittance to the Lord's Supper.

Sarah wrote meditations, prayers, several hymns, and an account of her conversion before her marriage to one Mr. Davy. She died around 1669, when she was just thirty-one years old.

She believed that true honor is found not in titles or things the world can bestow but in favor with God. She found contentment in God's presence and was spiritually nourished by Scripture reading, meditation, prayer, and worshiping with others at church. She wrote that her happiness was in knowing that Christ died for her, one sinner among many.

Sarah added a postscript to her book: "I know that my Redeemer liveth and that I will see him with these eyes. O that the time would come. But I will wait upon the Lord the days of my appointed time, till my change comes."[2]

Christianity is not a solitary journey along a desolate path, but a passage to Paradise in the company of others. Sarah was unable to reconcile her inner conflict until she prayed for and received support from a soul friend and church community. Many people are stranded on their way and confused about the way forward. Could you befriend them? Don't be wary of offering a hand to others, if that impulse stems from deep within. You are not called to work wonders but to be a channel for the compassionate Friend of all.

In the following readings from *Record of my Consolations and the Meditations of my Heart,* Sarah gives us insight into the rewards God gives to the patient and humble, and sings of the delights to be found in God's presence.

One Touch of Christ's Garment

"One more experience of the providence of God appeared unto me as an encouragement to trust in his mercy and to wait upon him by prayer for all things. I had at that time a distemper upon me of which I saw no hope of cure. Yet one day, particularly being in a serious meditation of the infinite goodness of the Lord toward me, the Lord was pleased to direct my eye upon a place of Scripture where I found the woman coming to the Lord, confessing that she had spent all she had to be cured of her infirmity, and one touch of Christ's garment had done it.

"From thence may not I come trembling, that have received so many testimonies of his love and tried so many medicines before I came unto the Lord or looked up to him for help? Then did I bewail my unprofitableness yet went unto the Lord in the language of the leper and said, 'Lord, if thou wilt thou canst make me clean,' who was not deaf to my poor request, but in some small time was graciously pleased as I may say without means wholly to clear me of it. This mercy carried . . . my heart more to praise the Lord then any yet I had received, who, notwithstanding all my weaknesses and sinfulness, was graciously pleased to follow me with many mercies."[3]

One Touch of Christ's Garment

The Lowly Soul, God's Dwelling Place

"Then was the Lord pleased in his gracious providence to remove me to a place in H. Sh. where I had much more advantage of means and helps for my poor soul, where the Lord was pleased to give me, through his grace, a little more insight into the mind of Christ, evidencing himself to be a God gracious and merciful, abundant in goodness, etc.

"I was filled with admiration to see the holy glorious God abase himself to so poor a wretchful creature as I then was. I cried out with earnest desires and longings after more of the knowledge of this God, but here I came under strong temptations. Satan was powerful in raising up of spiritual pride.

"But the Lord, whose goodness never failed me, did then take care of me. Thou, O Lord, who broughtest me out of the pit of despair, O suffer me not to climb up to the mount of presumption.

"Then was the Lord pleased in the tenderness of his love to convince me that the poor in spirit were the heirs of the kingdom, that the lowly soul was his habitation. Then I besought God, begging at the throne of grace for the assistance of his gracious Spirit, without which I could do nothing, and that he would humble me even to the dust, that so my soul might not lose the sight of that glory revealed in the face of Jesus Christ.

"This the Lord was graciously pleased to grant and sweetly bring me to see a riches in Christ Jesus and that this was more to be desired than all the treasures upon Earth."[4]

A Praising Soul

Lord, shall a heaven-born soul forget to sing
Eternal praises to her Lord and King?
Shall she be one that seemeth not to know
The hand from which her mercies still do flow?
O quicken, Lord, thy servant, O that she
May have her life all praises unto thee.

O 'tis a life of praises thou wouldst have,
Thy poor redeeméd ones return to thee.
Give, Lord, what thou art pleased from them to crave
Of thy own store, what thou accept'st must be.

Then, my dear Lord, I shall not cease to sing
The Song of Canaan unto Israel's king.

Though in a land so far and strange I be,
As destitute of what I would enjoy,
Let me by faith my native country see
And not forsake my treasure for a toy.
O blessed be thy name which still doth keep
My drowsy soul which else would ever sleep,

And lose its glorious comforts, sweet delights
Which in the presence of its Lord is found,
Those heavenly glories and transcendent sights
In which to empty souls grace doth abound.
O glorious grace let my soul still admire
And warm itself at this blest heavenly fire.

O shall I grieve that glorious Spirit which
is pleased to bow and condescend so low,
Thus to a poor unworthy sinful wretch.
How is it, Lord, that I thy grace should know
And that thou shouldest be pleased to look on me
So as redeem me from such misery?[5]

Reflection Questions

Scripture reassures us that God answers prayer. "Bless the Lord, O my soul, and do not forget all his benefits" (*Ps. 103:2*). Remember an instance in which God answered your prayer. Did you respond with gratitude? Think back across the last day. For what can you give gratitude to God now?

Scripture says, "Give thanks in all circumstances . . ." (*1 Thess. 5:18*). Find the hidden blessings in things that upset you.

Sarah was healed of an ailment after finally being led to pray to God for help. Is God your first or last resort in difficulty? Pray to turn to God more readily.

What is spiritual pride? How does it contrast with humility? What means do we have to guard against spiritual pride? Consider Davy's phrase "to empty souls grace doth abound."

Notes

1. Sarah Davy, *Heaven Realiz'd, or The Holy Pleasure of daily intimate Communion with God . . .* (London, 1670), p. 2. Elaine Hobby in *Virtue of Necessity: English Women's Writing*, 1646–1688 (London: Virago Press, 1988), p. 214, note 9, identifies "A.P.," the writer of the prefatory remarks to Davy's work, as the Baptist minister Anthony Palmer of Pinners' Hall, London. Skerpan-Wheeler quotes this identification. However, in the *Dictionary of National Biography*, s.v. "Palmer, Anthony," he is identified as an Independent minister who gathered a "Congregational" church and was personally "anabaptistically *inclined.*" From this, he cannot be classified with a certainty as "Baptist." In any case, it is clear that Sarah Davy was, as her text states (p. 21), "Congregationalist." (In England "Independent" churches were Congregational.)
2. Davy, *Heaven Realiz'd*, p. 151.
3. Ibid., p. 17.
4. Ibid., pp. 18–19.
5. Ibid., pp. 145–46. This hymn may be sung to the tune of Song 1 by Orlando Gibbons (1583–1625) found in *The Presbyterian Hymnal: Hymns, Psalms, and Spiritual Songs* (Louisville: Westminster/ John Knox Press, 1990), no. 385.

V

Mary Rich, 1625–1678

A Burning and a Shining Light

You may rub shoulders with the type any day at a trendy store: an irreverent society girl obsessed with her appearance. Her smile elates you but her snub is devastating. Don't dismiss her because she is rich, beautiful, and blows hot and cold. Rather, see her as a soul-in-training who has a long way to go. The Spirit ebbs and flows about her, and she may yet be transformed and do tremendous things for God. Here is the story of one such conversion.

Her chaplain praised Mary Rich, Countess of Warwick, as a "great lover of souls." But until her marriage into an influential and deeply religious family she was thought vain, inconsiderate, and obsessed with fine clothing. She was a superficial Christian who spent her time reading romances, attending the theater, and being seen in the company of other aristocrats at court.

Mary was born in Youghal, Ireland, in November 1625 to the Anglo-Irish couple Richard Boyle, First Earl of Cork, and his second wife, Catherine Fenton, Countess of Ranelagh. After her mother died when Mary was three, Mary and her sister Margaret were raised by Sir Randall and Lady Cleyton, a childless couple who loved them as their own. They educated Mary in French, needlework, etiquette, catechism, and the Bible. When she was about eleven, her father took her to Dorsetshire, England, and when she was thirteen or fourteen, informed her she was to marry James Hamilton (later Earl of Clanbrassil), a match he had decided on some years before.

Mary disliked James at first sight and refused him. Her father then took her to London and introduced her to many suitable wealthy men. But she was searching for romantic love and refused them too. Richard Boyle dismissed his unruly daughter to a farmhouse in the country.

Trusted Voices

There she fell in love with Charles Rich (later, Earl of Warwick), whom she married in a simple private ceremony on July 27, 1641, when she was fifteen years old. Mary and Charles had a daughter, Elizabeth, who died when she was about a year old. Mary found solace in the birth of their son, Charles (Lord Rich), and in raising the three daughters of her father-in-law's third marriage. They lived with her husband's family at Leighs Priory near Felsted, Essex.

Mary's in-laws were intensely Puritan: they expected prayer, Bible reading, soul-sharing, and twice daily attendance at the family chapel. Mary came into the household ignorant of the spiritual aspects of religion and was dead set against all of it.[1]

When her son, Charles, became seriously ill, she promised God that if her prayer for healing were granted, she would become a "new creature." To the doctor's astonishment, the boy's health improved. A while later, the family went away for two months; when they returned, they found Mary transformed.

Although Mary had been cool toward visiting ministers, she now sought them out and was reverent at worship. She turned to Anthony Walker, the family chaplain, as a spiritual mentor. Since the home teemed with people and she was expected to visit, she had to go outdoors to find solitude for prayer.

At Leighs she sought out the wilderness, a term in the 1600s that meant an area within a park or garden of trees often shaped as a labyrinth or maze. Like the contemporary form of prayer, this "labyrinth" was a system of patterns following a design. But we cannot tell whether Mary walked the maze in a meditative way. She repaired to her wilderness for prayer, reading Scripture and "good books," meditating, engaging in self-examination, and writing in her spiritual diary. She regularly consulted two "soul friends," and gave spiritual counsel to her servants and at least one friend, George Berkeley, for whom she wrote "Rules for a Holy Life."

Mary Rich was, observed Anthony Walker, "exuberant in charity." She built a special shelter nearby from which to distribute food to the poor of the neighboring area whom she fed in great numbers. She supported ministers whose parishes did not provide a living wage, foreigners who fled to England to escape persecution, and young students who needed books and clothing. She gave, said Anthony, with no noise. Those who wanted an excuse not to like her sniffed that her charity was excessive.

A Burning and a Shining Light

In May 1668, Mary wrote in her diary:

"5. In the morning, as soon as up, I retired into the wilderness to meditate; my meditation was sweet. Afterwards, read and prayed; my heart breathed after God in that prayer. All the afternoon, I was taken up with casting accounts. After supper, I committed my soul to God.

18. After dinner, was much taken up with doing works of charity for sick and distressed people.

22. In the morning, my lord went to London. As soon as he was gone, I retired into the wilderness to meditate; my meditation was sweet."[2]

Mary's husband, Charles, died in 1673; she died five years later. Entitled to a ceremonial funeral, she spurned custom and left directions for a modest one. In her will she gave generous legacies to her servants and to the neighborhood poor. Anthony Walker, her pastor and friend of thirty years, said she was faithful, kind, constant, unreserved, and unsuspicious. Mary Rich, he reflected, "would make people good by believing them to be so." As a Christian, he deemed her "complete in Christ," a model of piety, grace, and dignity for others.[3]

Mary once wrote a meditation after observing a candle used to light other candles. It "still gives as much light as it did before, and hath lost nothing by what it hath imparted unto them." Then she prayed: "O Lord . . .[may I] bring many others to know thee, not only with a general, but an [experiential], knowledge; which will make them say as I do that thou art good and dost good. O let me, by declaring what thou hast done for my soul, cause others to join with me in adoring thee for thy greatness and loving thee for thy goodness, that so we may magnify thy name together, and [that] I may be instrumental to impart light to others and be made a burning and a shining light myself."[4]

Mary went through an amazing transformation from lighthearted aristocrat to devout, mature woman. She never lost her strong will but allowed God to redirect her energy by lighting a self-giving flame within her heart. When God enters your heart, it is not to obliterate your personality but to transfigure it. Many people are dwelling in shadows and lonely corners. Will you reach out to God, that God may enable you to grasp the hands of others and draw them toward the peaceful Light?

Trusted Voices

Read how Mary Rich responded with compassion and prayer to a neighbor's request and reflect on the spiritual counsel she gave to a good friend. Learn how important it is to tend the garden of your soul. These passages are taken from her diary and her letter, "Rules for a Holy Life."

God Moved My Heart

"[June 9, 1668] . . . Had a woman come to me for another poor woman, that was on the Friday before, of a sudden, by the dead palsy,[5] struck speechless and one side quite dead; but having some sense, the woman that came to me asked her if she should come to me for something for her. She showed much satisfaction at her motion and pointed her to go. Upon hearing this, God was pleased much more than ordinary to move my heart to compassionate her; and after I had sent some palsy balsam[6] I retired and prayed to God to bless it to her and to restore her to her speech again.

"After dinner, the woman running much in my mind, I could not be quiet till I went to see her and got young Mr. Benson, the minister, to go with me. When I came to the door, the woman told me that, as soon as she had done all that I had ordered her to do, it pleased God to make her presently speak two or three words, by which she cried for mercy. When I came in, the woman prayed God to reward me; and after the minister had prayed with her, and in prayer my heart went out to God for mercy for her, she seemed mightily affected, which gave me much satisfaction.

"[June 11] . . . I also praised God for letting me hear this morning that a poor woman who had lain speechless for three days, and was by something which I sent her brought to speak again, was now also able to stir that leg that was struck dead. I begged also that God would be pleased to make me instrumental to save her life, which prayer God heard and restored her to life."[7]

Be Not a Stranger at Home

"As your friend, you must give me leave to give you not only good counsel, but my own experiences too, like nurses who feed their children nothing but what they have first themselves digested into milk, and to assure you that however the devil and wicked men may persuade you that religion will make you melancholy, yet I can assert from my own experience that nothing can give you that comfort, serenity, and composedness of mind as a pious and orderly-led life.

A Burning and a Shining Light

"This will free you from all those sad disquieting remorses and checks of conscience which follow an ill action, and give you that peace of God which passes all understanding and the continual feast of a good conscience. This will make you rejoice with joy unspeakable and full of glory. This will calm your desires and quiet your wishes, so as you shall find the consolations of God are not small. You will find you have made a happy exchange, having gold for brass and pearls for pebbles.

"For truly, my lord, I am, upon trial, convinced that all the pleasures of this world are not satisfactory. We expect a great deal more from them than we find. For pleasures die in their birth and therefore, as Bishop Hall says, are not worthy even to come into the bills of mortality. I must confess, for my own part, though I had as much as most people in this kingdom to please me and saw it in all the glories of the court, and was both young and vain enough to endeavor having my share in all the vanities thereof, yet I never found they satisfied me.

"God having given me a nature incapable of satisfaction in anything below the highest excellency, I never in all my life found real and satisfying comforts but in the ways of God, and I am very confident your lordship never will. Therefore I beseech you try this, and then I verily believe you will be of my opinion—that 'her ways are ways of pleasantness, and all her paths are peace.'[8]

"When you have spent what time you think fit in your recreations or visiting friends or receiving visits from them, then I would have you every day set some time apart for reading good books and meditation. Do not fear that a little time alone would make you melancholy, for the way not to be alone is to be alone, and you will find yourself never less alone than when you are so. For certainly, the God that makes all others good company, must needs be best himself.

"Be often in the profitable work of self-examination; be not a stranger at home, but pray Augustine's prayer: 'Lord, make me know thee and myself.' You will find the practice of this rule conduce much to the good of your soul. This will make you see what sin is most predominant and what grace is most weak and therefore had need be strengthened. It will keep sin from growing undiscerned by you. Remember, my lord, the best gardens have need often to be weeded or else they will soon be overrun, and the most delicate neat house must be often swept, or else there will be much dirt and dust in it."[9]

Reflection Questions

Mary's pastor commented that she made "people good by believing them to be so." Do you expect people to be at their spiritual best? Do you believe that expectations can affect others? Do you think Jesus exercised such spiritual intentions? Give an example.

Mary recommended setting time aside for spiritual reading and reflection. "You are what you eat," says a proverb. Are we also what we read?

A Reformed practice dating back to the Reformation has been to examine one's conscience in the evening before prayer. Why should we bother to "weed out our garden"?

Self-examination is a spiritual practice most of us experience as we pray in silent periods of confession during worship. It is a powerful tool for spiritual growth, based in Scripture (see *1 Cor. 11:28:* "Examine yourselves . . ."). To do so effectively, we pray for the Holy Spirit to shine on the shadows in our hearts that we may see our hidden flaws.

At the close of the day we review our interactions and conversations with others. Did I do or say something I regretted? Was I kind and loving? Recall specific instances. It may be helpful to "measure" yourself against a passage of Scripture.

The English Presbyterian Puritan Matthew Henry (1662–1714) once referred to James 3:8, meditating on the "tongue" as "full of deadly poison" yet also an instrument to bless God. Then he comments, "How have I used my tongue? It was designed to be my glory, but has it not been my shame?" "Have not I sometimes spoken unadvisedly, and said that in haste which at leisure I could have wished unsaid? Have not I said that, by which God's great name has been dishonoured, or my brother's good name reproached . . .?"[10]

Include your insights in your prayer of confession. For example, pray for forgiveness and for the grace to speak with better judgment and kindness.

Notes

1. Mary Rich, *Autobiography of Mary Countess of Warwick*, ed. with intro. and notes by T. Crofton Croker (London: Percy Society, 1848), p. 21.

2. Mary Rich, *Memoir of Lady Warwick: Also Her Diary from* A.D. *1666 to 1672* (London: Religious Tract Society, 1847), p.156.

3. Ibid., pp. 43, 50, 34.

4. Mary Rich, *Occasional Meditations* (London, 1678) 166–68.

5. "Dead palsy," a paralysis producing complete immobility; i.e., a stroke.

6. "Palsy balsam." One of the leading medical texts of the 1600s, *Praxis Medicinae universalis; Or A generall Practise of Physicke*, was compiled and written by Christopher Wirtzung and translated by Jacob Mosan (London, 1598). In the section titled "Of the Apoplexy or Dead Paulsey" (pp. 159–61), Wirtzung writes, "This disease is both very common, and very dangerous for old folks, especially if they have kept an immoderate diet before" (p. 159). Mary's "palsy balsam" may well have been made of several herbal preparations suggested by the German physician. The recipes are complex. Rich must have been skilled in herbal medicine.

7. Rich, *Memoir*, pp. 157–58. Diary entry.

8. Proverbs 3:17.

9. Rich, "Rules for a Holy Life," a letter written to George Berkeley, in Rich, *Memoir*, pp. 277–79.

10. Matthew Henry, *The Communicant's Companion* (Philadelphia: Presbyterian Board of Publication, n.d.), p. 94.

VI

Elisabeth West, fl. 1675–1709

My Mountain Stands Strong

Sometimes it seems as if all popular Christianity is about "Loving God 101." But some who progress may find their spiritual journey leading beyond the sweet pastures of the Shepherd into desolate paths and dark nights. Christ is still there but hidden so that believers may feel abandoned, just as Jesus did when he cried out from the cross.

One Scottish woman found that friends, Scripture, prayer, and public worship enabled her to endure her desert journey. When God leads you to spiritual growth through rough times, take heart from the transformation of Elisabeth West.

Elisabeth West dreamed of heaven as a place where she would be dressed in fine clothes and everything would be "brave and bonny." Being good was the only way to heaven, her mother warned, so the Scottish girl became devout. She thought her parents were not religious, however, and berated her father for not leading family worship every day.

She prayed regularly but had naïve views. "The truth is," she wrote in her journal, "I thought there was not a difficulty in all the way to heaven." She was puzzled that some found religion gloomy. "I can see nothing but joy. I was with David singing, 'My mountain stands strong; I shall never be moved.' "[1] George Meldrum, pastor of Tron Kirk, Edinburgh, Elisabeth's parish church, encouraged her to keep a journal. She thought this was odd until another pastor also suggested it.

Elisabeth began to write in 1694. Her journal, published as a memoir in 1766, went on to become popular and influential in Great Britain and the United States. She gives only a few biographical details: that she was a member of the Church of Scotland, lived in Edinburgh for a number of years, and worked as a maid.

One Friday Elisabeth was worshiping in Tron Kirk. She found the sermon so tedious and boring that she almost left before the end of the service. But not wanting to set a bad example she remained and watched as the minister baptized some children. All of a sudden a dog bit her hard on the leg. She was about to discover why some people found religion gloomy: she would have a fierce time of it.

Although she felt oppressed by a sense of God's absence, Elizabeth kept August 9, 1694, as a fast day in preparation for her first communion. The next day she wrote a covenant prayer, which concludes: ". . . if thou be my portion, I have enough. I here this day promise to renounce all lusts and idols, and give my heart to thee; all which I shall seal tomorrow at thy table."[2] Elisabeth became a communicant member of the Church of Scotland on August 11.

For a brief time afterward she was full of joy and found spiritual life easy. "What can make a Christian's way difficult!" she enthused.[3] Several months later on Christmas night, as she meditated on a sermon, God surprised Elisabeth with a strong sense of the divine presence. Soon afterward she fell "into an extraordinary deadness of spirit. I was . . . deserted. I [knew] not what to do."[4] Distressed, she turned to her friends but found no one with whom she could talk.

Things got worse. She began to fall asleep while praying. Satan assailed her when she tried to pray, suggesting that there was no God; that the Bible was not God's word; that ministers were seducers, not servants; and that spiritual practices were useless.

After five difficult months, Elisabeth found some relief while reading John Bunyan's *Grace Abounding to the Chief of Sinners*. On April 12, 1695, God drew near and consoled her. Days later, she renewed her baptismal covenant and briefly felt joy, but spiritual deadness soon returned. She slept when she wanted to pray and warred with unbelief, self-conceit, and self-centeredness.

Elisabeth's spiritual trials continued thirteen years: "My winter season was lengthened out," she observed.[5] How did she endure such a long period of spiritual aridity and struggle, what seems to have been a dark night of the spirit? God brought her occasional solace through conversation with friends and prayer, through the comfort of Scripture impressed on her heart by the Holy Spirit, and through public worship, especially sermons and the sacrament of the Lord's Supper.

Elisabeth devoted whole chapters of her journal to recalling sermons she heard and her reflections on them, and gave long accounts of journeys to area kirks for "sacraments," eucharistic festivals that ran three or more days.[6] Communion was so integral to her spirituality that she used the term "communion feast" as a metaphor for an open door in prayer. Throughout her long spiritual winter she continued to read Scripture, to meditate on it, and to pray.

On Sunday, April 3, 1709, Elisabeth sat down at the communion table. She was feeling "in a very bad frame," yet a tremendous sense of expectation swept over her. The pastor, Mr. Bird, served the elements, saying: "Believer, maybe thou art saying, 'I cannot find what I expected.' But I must tell thee, he hath a better dish and cup provided for thee than what thou hast in hand."[7]

With these words, Christ came to her with extraordinary power and delivered her from her long spiritual night. Elisabeth compared the experience of desertion with her new sense of God's nearness: "O but this was a sweet and comfortable time to me! For I lived an heaven upon earth in comparison of what storms I had undergone . . . where I was racked and tortured . . . but now there was a great delivery."

"I compared myself to a ship that had been long at sea, and by reason of many storms, was all broken in pieces but yet, broken as it was, the wise Master Pilot, the Lord Jesus Christ, brought this tossed vessel to a safe harbor in himself."[8]

During her difficult spiritual journey, Elisabeth was transformed from a child who thought that the path to God was carefree to a follower of Christ, shouldering her cross. As her story shows, this process is often unpleasant: Elisabeth felt like a ship shattered to pieces by numerous storms. We too may face abrupt encounters that mark the end of childlike faith and signal periods of purification and rigorous spiritual growth. May we be humble and teachable in the face of all that happens to us and hold tightly to God; the voyage may be rough, but the haven is sure.

The following passages are from Elisabeth West's spiritual memoir. She describes her personal struggles in approaching Christ in the Lord's Supper and shares a memorable dream. Perhaps her experiences will help you place yours in perspective.

What Is Thy Request, Queen Esther?

"It pleased the Lord to give me another occasion of renewing my former engagements, which were dreadfully broken on my part. I saw that I could not walk with the Lord; therefore I must not let any opportunity pass of lending myself to the Lord. I also was at the time labouring under the power of a body of sin and death, and saw no remedy but in Christ.

"There was word of a communion at Preston-pans, at the hearing of which, there arose a vehement desire in my heart to be there, I having experienced the manifestations of his presence formerly at such occasions, that called me to that place; also inward corruptions and outward dispensations of providence. I was persuaded I had the Lord's call to go there from these two Scriptures: 'Seek and ye shall find, knock and it shall be opened unto you.' The other was, 'Follow the Lamb, wherever he goeth.'[9]

"I met with some oppositions which had a tendency to hinder me to go there, but the Lord overcame them all. I cannot but remark two of these hindrances: in the first place I had a sore and vehement pain of the toothache, which distressed me mightily, so that I was capable of nothing but crying of pain. There was none that thought I would be so cruel to myself as to adventure on such a journey tomorrow, and yet I was firmly resolved I would be there. The other hindrance was that the weather was extraordinarily boisterous, with great rains, terrible winds, fire-slaughts and thunder, so that I thought the house would blow down about me that night.

"On the morrow when I awaked, the pain of my tooth was quite gone from me, which I reckoned no small mercy, but still the wind continued loud and bitter, which made all the family plead with me to forbear my going there.

"But I gave a deaf ear to them all, and away I came to Preston-pans. It being Saturday morning, the way was very pleasant to me, though otherwise unpleasant. When I met with the poor women with their burdens of coal and salt on their backs coming to the market of Edinburgh, then I thought the badness of the weather does not hinder these from their earthly market. O what a fool would I have been, if anything should have hindered me from the heavenly market!

"When I came to the place, O how sweet and refreshful were these Saturday sermons to me! Mr. John Moncrief was on Exodus 20:24. 'In all places where I record my name, I will come unto thee and bless thee.' He observed that ordinances were trysting places between Christ and his people, and whoever there was that had been trysting Christ to come to this communion, if they were come to keep the tryst on their part, Christ was also come to keep it on his part. He told us of four ways that Christ was coming to keep tryst with his people. ·

"First, he was coming as a merchant, to see what his poor people wanted, with all the wares of heaven, and now, O communicants, what will ye buy this day? Secondly, he was coming as a physician, to sick folk; and I must tell one and all of you, there is not one among you all, but ye are sick and that dangerously, of a sickness you must all die of it, if you employ not this physician. And for your encouragement, I tell you, there is not one in heaven but what was sick of this disease, and he healed them all perfectly. Thirdly, he is coming as a king, and will ye not open your hearts to receive [him]? Fourthly, he is coming as a suitor, to court a bride for himself and will ye refuse to marry the king of glory?

"Every one of these things were sweeter to me than another. When sermons were ended, I, being a stranger in the place, had great difficulty to get quarters, but when all my hope was past, how wonderfully did providence direct me to a place where I was better entertained than I expected?

"On Sabbath morning, being October 9, 1697, I was big with expectation that all would be well; and when I came to the kirk, I had no will to go to the first table, lest I should be deprived of a seat afterwards. But about an hour before the sermon began, the minister of that place, Mr. George Andrew, came to the kirk in his night-gown, and seeing but two persons at the first table, he uttered this lamentable expression, 'Will our Lord Jesus get but two brides today? Woe's our heart, we have enough of weights on us, though ye add not this to the rest.' The words were scarce out of his mouth when the table was full and I was there among the rest.

"I was no sooner set down at it but that word came with light, life and power, 'What is thy request, Queen Esther? And it shall be granted thee.'[10] I had a sweet time at the table before the work began. Mr. George Andrew was on Matthew, 'Come to the marriage, for all things are ready,'[11] where he made a free offer of Christ to all that would come and receive him on his own terms, in which place I took him to witness, the heaven and earth, the sun that shined bright in my face, to witness, that then it was a sealed bargain betwixt Christ and me, for I was made willing with the offer.

"When the minister came to serve the first table, he came with that word in his mouth, 'What is thy request, Queen Esther? And it shall be granted thee.' O then my heart cried out, my request is that the Bridegroom's image may be stamped on my heart presently.

"Come, Lord, here is a temple for thee to dwell in such as it is. But do thou [come] to it, as thou did to the temple, whip out all the buyers and sellers and everything that defileth it. I have great idols, unmortified corruptions, who, Haman-like, strive to overcome me. O make me more holy than ever I was before, that the image of my Lord and Bridegroom may appear in my converse with others in the world.

"Let me have as near a conformity to thee as ever any attained to. I this day request for more light in reading thy holy word, for as yet it is the darkest book I ever read upon. I also request for my poor parents, as formerly, and all my Christian acquaintances, ministers and people, and for our land in general, and that the gospel may never depart from Scotland. Come purge thy house of everything that hinders thy appearance among the golden candlesticks. O Lord, grant me greater degrees of humility, both outward and inward, for I find my self-conceit sometimes like to overcome me. I here this day promise, as in thy sight, to stand to thy interest, though persecution should arise, and to lay down my life, if thou call for it.

"Come, Lord, tie both me and my resolutions to thyself fast, that I slide not back in trying times and be not like that son that said he would go to work in the vineyard but went not. I must confess to the glory of God, I got great liberty in seeking all these things, both in public and secret [prayer].

"O but it was a comfortable day to me, wherein my interest in Christ was as visible to me as if it had been written in golden letters before my eyes! It is impossible for the tongues of men or angels to declare the joy and comfort I experienced, and, wherein I gave myself to the Lord and in testimony thereof, I take myself to witness, and all in heaven and earth, that I am not my own, but the Lord's.

"Written and subscribed at Preston-pans, October 9, 1697. Elisabeth West."[12]

O Harlot, Hear the Word of the Lord
"[1698] There is one thing I have to observe from the Lord's way with me in my journey heavenward: it is up the brae and down the brae [up the hill and down the hill]. The whole way I was the last day was, as it were, upon the top of the

brae, and now, on the back of this, I must down the brae and enter a new combat with my predominant sin again. Alas! My predominant sin was like my shadow; it never left me. O the confusion that in a short time it brought me under! Till at last I concluded my spots were not the spots of God's children, for I thought I was one of the most abominable creatures that ever was born.

"One night I dreamed a dream, and thought I saw a woman going through the streets in the most vile and loathsome condition imaginable, she being a monster of uncleanness. She was crying, 'Will none have pity upon me?' I looked upon her but was forced to put my hands on my eyes so that I might not see her again, and I said to her, 'Woman, thou art such an object that none would pity.' With this I awaked and began to think on my dream. I thought: What if a king's son were coming by, and seeing this object that none would pity, should take her into his coach and wash her himself? This would be thought wonderful kindness.

"Immediately the sixteenth chapter of Ezekiel came into my mind, and in a little time I saw myself to be an object of a more heinous nature by far than the woman was; and yet the King of glory came by himself and pitied me when I was cast out into the open field.

"For many days the impression of this woman went not out of my mind, and many sweet meditations I got from it, all which consisted in these three: first, what I was by nature; secondly, what Christ had done for me; thirdly, what I had proved and was like to prove after all this love.

"The more I read in this chapter, I still saw my own picture the more drawn to the life, but especially how ungrateful I proved to so kind a Lord, and had taken his jewels, and his fine embroidered garments, which he gave me to cover my nakedness, and had bestowed them upon the Canaanites and Amorites, my strange lovers; my idols and predominants [sins] got all the earrings and jewels and love tokens I got from my kind Husband; and not that they forced them from me, but I gave them deliberately.

"Then went out that sentence against me, 'O harlot, harlot, hear the word of the Lord.'[13] . . . I thought myself unparallelable for abominations of all sorts. In the meantime, when I was thus exercised, I heard of a communion to be at Dalkeith. I was resolved to lie about the pool's mouth[14] with all my grievous maladies, and also inquire: What might be the cause, why I was so dragged and tormented with the corruptions of my heart? I went there but durst not approach to the table, I was such an unclean beast.

"When all the work was over, I retired alone where I received a strong conviction for neglecting the duty of communicating. The conviction came by way of question, and it was thus: 'What brought you to this place? Had you any errands? If you had any, why came ye not to the King with them? And, if ye had none, why came ye here to disturb my people and only to hear bulk?' With that my heart began to melt, and in his sight I could appeal, that I came not there without an errand, and that the weary sighs and groans I was giving could testify that these brought me to this place, to see if I could find out the cause why I was in these confusions.

"I must acknowledge that the Lord was very gracious to me in this place, and though I was not at the table, yet I bless his name I was taken into the party, where I got some discoveries of his goodness and condescension, and the cause of my perpetual confusion. In the same place, he made me resolve that the first occasion of that nature I should not neglect it, as I have done this, though all the devils in hell and corruptions of my own heart should oppose it."[15]

Reflection Questions

Reformed people have long made covenant renewal a central aspect of their spiritual life. How could reaffirming your baptismal covenant strengthen you to endure a long period of spiritual dryness?

Consider reaffirming your baptismal covenant using resources provided in the *Book of Common Worship* (Louisville: Westminster John Knox Press, 1993), pp. 464–88; Keith Beasley-Topliffe, *Surrendering to God: Living the Covenant Prayer* (Brewster, Mass.: Paraclete Press, 2001), p. 1.; or Richard Alleine's covenant prayer in Diane Karay Tripp, ed., *Prayers from the Reformed Tradition* (Louisville: Witherspoon Press, 2001), p. 153.

Elisabeth was nourished by the Lord's Supper and believed that this sacrament is a meeting place between Christ and his people. Do you feel nourished at the Table?

Consider that Christ's presence may strengthen you even though you don't feel his nearness. What do you think Jesus meant when he said, "I have food to eat that you don't know about" (*John 4:32*)?

Elisabeth once immersed herself in Ezekiel 16 for days. "Every verse in this chapter had an express language to me," she said. Is there a chapter of the Bible that speaks to your heart now? Consider the practice of *lectio divina,* the Latin phrase for "spiritual reading," letting Scripture penetrate your heart, contemplating phrases that draw your attention, praying the Scripture and resting silently in God's presence.[16]

Elisabeth once felt God rebuke her when she went to worship but did not receive the sacrament of the Lord's Supper. This changed her heart. Are you open to God's correction? Isn't correction a primary tool for growth?

Notes

1. Elisabeth West, *Memoirs, or Spiritual Exercises of Elisabeth West: Written by her own Hand* (Glasgow, 1766), p. 8.
2. Ibid., p. 7. In 1694 she learned the discipline of personal covenanting with God: an affirmation of the baptismal covenant undertaken in preparation for feasting at the Lord's Table for the first time. The focus of the ritual was surrendering oneself unconditionally to God. Once made the covenant was renewed often, particularly on one's birthday, at the beginning of the new year, during days of fasting and prayer, and each time one participated in the Lord's Supper. The English Presbyterian Puritan Joseph Alleine (1634–1668) popularized covenant renewal. Anglicans, Reformed people, and, later, Methodists had a tradition of writing out a covenant prayer as a sacred document and signing and dating it each time they affirmed their intention to be wholly for the Lord and no other. The practice is described in Joseph Alleine,
    An Alarme to Unconverted Sinners (London, 1672), pp. 136ff; also, see Keith Beasley-Topliffe, *Surrendering to God: Living the Covenant Prayer* (Brewster, Mass.: Paraclete Press, 2001).
3. West, *Memoirs,* p. 8.
4. Ibid., p. 13.
5. Ibid., p. 140.
6. See Leigh Eric Schmidt, *Holy Fairs: Scottish Communions and American Revivals in the Early Modern Period* (Princeton: Princeton University Press, 1989).
7. West, *Memoirs,* p. 164.
8. Ibid., p. 165.
9. Matthew 7:7; Revelation 14:4.
10. Esther 5:3.
11. Matthew 22:4.
12. West, *Memoirs,* pp. 41–44.
13. Ezekiel 16:35.
14. See John 5:1–9.
15. West, *Memoirs,* pp. 54–55.
16. See: Fr. Luke Dysinger, O.S.B., "Accepting the Embrace of God: The Ancient Art of Lectio Divina," in *Lord, Teach Us to Pray—A Guide to Prayer* (Louisville, KY: Presbyterian Church [U.S.A.], Office of Spiritual Formation, n.d.). Dysinger's article is also available online at www.valyermo.com/ld-art.html.

VII

Abigail Ammapoo (d. 1710), Abiah Paaonit (d. 1712),
Jerusha Ohquanhut (1697–1714)

Preaching and Praying Women

I have lived near Amish people much of my life. When I moved away from north central Indiana, I sorely missed the Amish. Spiritual peace and freedom shine from many of their faces. "English" (non-Amish) faces seldom reflect such serenity. Three Native American women born in the 1600s radiated faith to others. One routinely prayed for her enemies. Another, though quite poor, gave to others who were still poorer, and the third demonstrated a trust in God that was stronger than her fear.

Abigail Ammapoo, Abiah Paaonit, and Jerusha Ohquanhut were three Christian Native Americans who lived on Martha's Vineyard, Massachusetts, and belonged to the Pawkunnawkutt federation, a branch of the Wamponoags. The women read the Bible, catechisms, and devotional books in their own language, belonged to churches that promoted literacy, valued women and provided them with leadership roles, and enjoyed the ministry of Native American pastors.[1]

No writing by the women survives. But Experience Mayhew, a Congregational lay missionary, published accounts of each in his book, *Indian Converts* (1727).[2]

Abigail Ammapoo, who lived in Christiantown near North Tisbury, was a recognized teacher of her children, grandchildren, and others and may have provided religious instruction to new converts. One of her resources may have been an Algonkian pamphlet titled "The Belief," which stressed three maxims of piety:

1. "The one most high God, who is the Father, and the Son, and the Holy Spirit, must be my God, and I must make it the main intention of my life to please him with all holy obedience and submission unto him, and be afraid of every thing which his light in my soul shall condemn as an evil thing.

2. A glorious Christ, who is the eternal Son of God, incarnate and enthroned in our Blessed Jesus, is the Redeemer of mankind, unto whose great sacri-

fice I must repair for acceptance with God. And under his conduct, I am to expect a complete happiness for my immortal soul, to which he will restore my body when he shall come to judge the world.

3. Out of respect unto God and his Christ, I must heartily love my neighbour and for ever do unto other men as I must own it is reasonable for them to do unto me."[3]

Abiah Paaonit of Chilmark was a prominent lay leader in her community. James P. Ronda believes she was a "discourser," a lay preacher who led family worship and preached when the regular pastor was absent. She may well have been a deacon. The globe-trotting English lawyer Thomas Morton observed female Congregational deacons among Native Americans: "There is amongst these people a Deaconess made of the sisters, that uses her gifts at home in an assembly of her sex, by way of repetition, or exhortation; such is their practice." He also noted that all pastors, elders, and deacons might preach.[4] Abiah had a particular ministry to Native American women and was always ready to lay aside domestic work to edify and "administer grace to the hearers."

Jerusha Ohquanhut made her home in Gay Head, a town consisting of fifty-eight wigwams and frame houses in 1712.[5] When she was fifteen years old, she sought admission to the Gay Head Indian Congregational Church, established around 1666 by the Native American pastor Mittark.[6]

Mayhew says she gave "good evidence of a work of grace on her soul," referring to a ritual by which churches received new members. Cotton Mather, a contemporary who occasionally worshiped at the Native American churches of Martha's Vineyard, gives an eyewitness account: "The person to be admitted stands forth in the midst of the assembly, and first makes a declaration of his knowledge, and sometimes desires information in things most arduous and doubtful. . . . And then he gives an account of experience he has had, of convictions, awakenings and comforts, in which they are large and particular. After which (much counsel and exhortation to remain steadfast in the faith and ways of the Lord, being given them by their pastor and elder) they are admitted."[7]

Abigail, Abiah, and Jerusha all subscribed to a faith centered on surrender to God and love of neighbor. They embodied Mary's contemplation and Martha's service. Does your abandonment to God lead you to nourish others in body and soul? Is your service rooted in prayer? Service without love provides meager nourishment. Love without service doesn't bother to set a place for others at the table. Will you allow God to bring you into balance?

The following readings are Experience Mayhew's brief biographical accounts of Abigail, Abiah, and Jerusha, as found in his book, *Indian Converts*. They focus on the women's faith, spiritual experience, and service to those in their communities.

Abigail Ammapoo, a "Diligent Instructor"
"This Abigail was the daughter of a petty sachem [tribal chief] of Home's Hole, called Cheshchaamog, and a sister of that Caleb Cheshchaamog, who took a degree in Harvard College in the year 1665. When she became a woman, she was married to Wunnannauhkomun, a godly minister. And though she was esteemed worthy to be a wife to such a husband, yet she made not a public profession of religion until after the gathering of the first Indian church on Martha's Vineyard, in the year 1670.

"She was taught to read while young and made a good improvement of that advantage, till by a scald in her face, she in a great measure lost her sight within a few years after she was first married.

"While her husband lived, she used to pray in the family in his absence, and frequently gave good counsel to her children.

"After she lived so long with her husband that the eldest of the three daughters which she had by him had become a mother, he died and left her a widow, but just as he was going out of the world, desiring his wife and daughters to tell him what petitions he should put up to God for them before he took his leave of them, the mother, her daughters joining with her in it, requested him to pray for spiritual blessings for her and them, which he did accordingly.

"Being thus left a widow, she lived in that estate the greatest part of her time after, for though she after some years married again, yet her husband soon dying, she chose not to marry after this but lived with her children and used to pray with them, and frequently gave many good instructions to them, as two of them yet living do testify.

"As she prayed much at other times, so she made God her refuge in an evil day, calling on him without fainting until he had mercy on her. And experiencing the mercy of God herself, she was very merciful to the poor, being, according to her capacity, ready to distribute and willing to communicate to them.

"She delighted much in going to the house of God and would scarce ever stay from meeting unless there were some very necessary occasion for it.

"She was a diligent instructor of her grandchildren, as well as of her own, earnestly exhorting them to love and fear God, and believe in Jesus Christ their only Savior; and lived to see some good effects of her pious endeavors in this way. Nor did she neglect to instruct and exhort other ignorant persons.[8]

"When she prayed, she was careful not to forget her enemies and would seldom fail of putting up some good petitions for them, and as she prayed for them, so she sought opportunities to do good to them and would sometimes say that that was the way in which people should heap coals of fire on the heads of them that hated them.

"She often spoke of this world as none of our resting place, and of herself and others as strangers and pilgrims in it. But of heaven she used to talk as a place of excellent glory where God the Father, Son, and Holy Spirit dwell, and from whence the holy angels come to minister to the saints on the earth, and to which they would at their death convey them. And of death she would sometimes speak as the hand of God, by which his people were removed into a better place than this world is, and would also call it a ferryman, by which we have our passage out of this life into the next.

"And she was herself careful to abstain from sin, so she was also a serious and sharp reprover of it, and used to call it the way to hell and damnation.

"She was long sick before she died, and though she underwent much pain in that time, yet she bore it with patience and resignation, being full of heavenly discourses, and calling often on God her Savior.

"One of her daughters, who, I hope, is a pious woman, affirms that being much broken by her rest by tending her mother night and day in her sickness, and being herself not well, her mother desired her to lie down and try to get a little sleep before it was well light on the morning of the day on which she died, but that telling her she was afraid she would suffer for want of help if she did so, her mother told her that God would take care of her.

"But this argument not prevailing with her to lie down, she, as she sat in the room drowsy, with her eyes well nigh shut, suddenly saw a light which seemed to her brighter than that of noonday.

"Looking up, she saw two bright shining persons standing in white raiment at her mother's bedside, who, on her sight of them, with the Light attending them, immediately disappeared, and that hereupon saying something to her mother of what she had seen, she replied, 'This is what I said to you, God taketh care of me.' She also, as I am informed, told another person before she died that her guardians were already come for her.

"She, just before departed this life, prayed earnestly to God for all her children and offspring, as her first husband did before he died, nor did she now forget to pray for others, and even for her enemies.

"And having thus called on the Lord, she presently after committed her soul into the hands of her Redeemer, and so expired.

"I was long acquainted with the person of whom these things are related, and always esteemed her a very godly woman.

"The account given by her daughter of what she saw before her mother died, being alone with her, she related soon after her death, and still maintains the truth of it."[9]

Abiah Paaonit, a Gifted Woman
"This woman was the eldest daughter of good Deacon Jonathan Amos and Rachel his wife, who, though they had no son, yet had a great blessing in their children, the most of them proving very pious persons.

"These godly parents of this Abiah took care to teach her to read when she was a child, and did otherwise well instruct her, so that she was a person of good knowledge in the things of God, and was, I think, from her very childhood, a sober and religious person.

"Elisha Paaonit, a minister, was her second husband, as she was his second wife, and they were both very happy in the marriage in which they were joined. She was a meet help unto him, did much reverence him, and took great care of him, keeping his apparel whole and in good order, his linen clean and neat, and carried herself in all respects towards him as a minister's wife should do.

"She joined herself as a member in full communion to the Indian church here while she was but a young woman, and she ever afterwards behaved herself as a person in church relation is obliged to do, adorning the doctrine of God her Savior in all things. Only one failing she was guilty of: she was too apt to be offended and to resent any injury which she received higher than she should have done. But then she would be easily satisfied and reconciled to the person that wronged her or which she supposed to have done so.

"She was remarkable for her love to the house and ordinances of God, for no light thing could hinder or detain her from an attendance on them. And when she was at them, she appeared to be most devout and serious, being often much affected at public prayers, sermons, and sacraments.

"She was well known to be a praying woman or else should not have been mentioned as a pious one. She prayed constantly in her family in her husband's absence, and often with sick women and children when there were occasions for it. Yea, in such esteem was she for the gift as well as the spirit of prayer wherewith the Holy Ghost had favored her, that when there was any special occasion for prayer where any number of women were met together without any men with them, as at women's travails,[10] etc., she, if among them, was commonly the person pitched upon to be their mouth to God to make known their requests to him.

"She was very observable for her forwardness to entertain religious discourses and her ability to manage them to the edification of those with whom she conversed. And though she was a woman of a commendable industry, yet if any of her neighbors came in to visit her, she would ordinarily lay her work aside that she might sit and discourse with them. And her discourses on such occasions were not vain and frothy, but such as were good for the use of edifying and might administer grace to the hearers.

"She was kind to her neighbors' bodies as well as to their souls, for though she was but a poor woman, yet she often distributed part of the little she had to such as she thought were in more want than she was.

Preaching and Praying Women

"She died of a consumption under which she languished several months before it put an end to her life. But as her outward man decayed, so her inward man was renewed day by day.

"She was in the former part of her illness rather disconsolate than joyful. She did not seem to be assured of her own personal interest in the great and good things, the existence whereof she doubtless by faith realized; and now she was very diligent in her endeavors to make her calling and election sure, calling often and earnestly upon God, that for Jesus Christ's sake he would pardon all her sins and be reconciled to her, discoursing very seriously about the things of God and another world. But what in particular the expressions were which she used, those who were with her do not so well remember as to undertake to relate, though they affirm the same to have been very edifying.

"As she drew nearer to her end, she appeared more joyful than she had formerly been, and there was one thing which happened not very long before she died that seemed somewhat to affect her.

"She being still able to sit up and go out when she was minded to do so, she once late in the night went out as she had hitherto sometimes done. (Our Indians go out much more in times of sickness than English people do.) But during the little time of her staying abroad, she was very suddenly refreshed with a light shining upon and about her, which she thought to be brighter than the sun at noonday. Being filled with admiration at this marvelous light, and looking upwards to see if she could discern from whence it came, she saw, as she thought, as it were, a window open in the heavens and a stream of glorious light issuing out from thence, and lighting upon her, which, while she admired it, in the twinkling of an eye disappeared.

"This account she presently gave to her husband, from whom I had it presently after the thing happened. She related the same also to some other credible persons yet living, who still remember the story, as it is here set down.

"What notice ought to have been taken of this phenomenon I shall not undertake to declare, but shall leave to the judgment of the judicious. But the woman herself who saw this light was somewhat affected at what she had seen, and diverse times spoke of it as some little glimpse of the glory of the heavenly world with which God had been pleased to favor her. She thought she had seen some rays of that glorious light which the saints in light do enjoy.

"But however it was as to this, she had in some of the last days of her life a more sure and certain discovery of the loving kindness of God to her soul, than any which such a light appearing to the eyes of her body could afford her. She had such foretastes of the joys of the heavenly world as made her heartily willing and desirous to leave this, and having experienced such a mercy, she comforted her relations whom she was to leave behind her, and earnestly exhorted them to go on to seek the Lord their God, and to be sure never to depart from him.

"Her last words were, 'O Lord, I beseech thee be gracious to my soul.' "[11]

Jerusha Ohquanhut, Woman of Faith
"This Jerusha Ohquanhut was a daughter of Peter Ohquanhut and Dorcas his wife, the said Peter being one of the present pastors of the Indian church on the west end of Martha's Vineyard.

"Her religious parents taught her to read and say her catechism while she was but young. They also taught her to call upon God when she was but a little girl, and she seemed very sober while she was but a child, and used to pray according to the instruction given her. Nor was she, as she did appear, addicted unto any vice, but carried herself well and was very obedient to her parents.

"When she was scarcely fifteen years old, her father endeavoring to pass the sound in a canoe, was taken by a French privateer and carried away. But whither, neither his own family nor any other could tell.

"At this mishap, this daughter of his (as well as the rest of his family and others) was exceeding troubled, but did at the same time encourage herself and the rest of her relations in the power, goodness, and providence of God, and expressed her dependence on him for the preservation and safe return of her father in his good time.

"She now put her friends in mind how God delivered Daniel out of the lion's den, and the three children out of the fiery furnace into which they were cast; and from thence inferred how easy a thing it was with God to set her father at liberty and bring him home to his family again.

"Having such a faith, she exercised the same in fervent prayer for her father's return, and her mother, perceiving that she was now very constant and earnest in her secret devotions, and knowing that she had been long used to call on the Lord, did sometimes invite and persuade her to pray in the family, there being none but themselves and little children in it. Nor was she at a loss how to express herself pertinently in the duty, but prayed like one that was used to it, as indeed she was and had for a long time been.

"In these addresses to heaven she prayed with much affection and ordinarily with tears,[12] enforcing her petitions with proper arguments taken out of the word of God, which she was no stranger to. Nor did she fail of mentioning her father's case in any of the prayers thus sent to God by her. And while she was thus earnest with God for the return of her father, he put in the hearts of the French to release him and set him on shore, who, being at liberty, got home to his family at Gay Head in about a month after he was taken.

"This young woman on the news of her father's return, and being already come as far as the next town, was so exceedingly affected, as for the present to fall into a swoon. But being in a short time recovered out of it, she expressed her great joy and thankfulness to God for his great goodness therein manifested.

"Not long after this she signified her intentions to her parents of renewing her covenant with God, and asking an admission to the table of the Lord. And being encouraged by them so to do, did it accordingly. And giving good evidences of a work of grace on her soul, was by the church readily admitted when she was but very little above fifteen years of age. Nor did this young woman ever by any miscarriage bring reproach on religion or the church whereof she was a member.

"As she appeared to be a very pious person in the time of her health, so she did in the time of that sickness also whereof she died, she then behaving herself as became an heir of God's eternal kingdom. I shall conclude my account of her with the last words she spake before she died, which being penned by her father, to whom, with the rest of her friends, she spake them, were in writing delivered to me, and they are these:

" 'My father, these are my last words to you, now in my end: worship God fervently, and be not much troubled for me, for as for me, I'm going to my heavenly Father. Serve God therefore with greater diligence and fervency than you used while I was well in health. And all of you my other friends, whom I know to have loved me, and who are also beloved of me, if you are sorry for my leaving of you, seek for me with Jesus Christ and there you shall find me, and with him we shall see one another for ever.' "[13]

Reflection Questions

A Puritan Indian teaching tool emphasized making pleasing God the main intention of one's life. What is your basic intention? How could you remind yourself of it? How do you live it out?

Abigail Ammapoo "prayed without fainting until [God] had mercy on her." Read Matthew 15:21–28 or Luke 18:1–8. When God is silent, do you give up or do you persevere in prayer?

Abiah Paaonit graciously received visitors and laid aside her work to converse with them. Listening to others is a great gift, but few of us do it well. Consider how you could improve giving others undivided attention.

Reformed people have long considered thanksgiving for answered prayer important. Jerusha Ohquanhut thanked God with great joy for the safe return of her father. Read Luke 17:11–19. Are you one who returns gratitude to God?

Notes

1. For a discussion of Native American culture encountered by Puritans that included matrilineal sociopolitical organization, women leaders, shamans, "love-doctors," and tradeswomen, see Robert Steven Grumet, "Sunksquaws, Shamans, and Tradeswomen: Middle Atlantic Coastal Algonkian Women During the 17th and 18th Centuries," in *Women and Colonization: Anthropological Perspectives*, ed. Mona Etienne and Eleanor Leacock (New York: Praeger Publishers, 1980), pp. 43–62.
2. Experience Mayhew, *Indian Converts: Or, Some Account of the Lives and Dying Speeches of a Considerable Number of the Christianized Indians of Martha's Vineyard* (London, 1727).
3. Cotton Mather, *India Christiana* (Boston, 1721), pp. 53–54.
4. James P. Ronda, "Generations of Faith: The Christian Indians of Martha's Vineyard," *William and Mary Quarterly*, Third Series, 38 (1981): 383. Thomas Morton (d. 1646), *New English Canaan* (Amsterdam, 1637), p.173.
5. Ives Goddard and Kathleen J. Bragdon, *Native Writings in Massachusett*, Pt. 1 (Philadelphia: The American Philosophical Society, 1988), p. 7.
6. Ronda, "Generations of Faith," 373.
7. Mather, *India Christiana*, pp. 39–40.
8. This may imply that Abigail Ammapoo was also a discourser and deacon. Mayhew seems reluctant to state the full status of the women.
9. Mayhew, *Indian Converts*, pp. 148–51.
10. Apparently, a group of women gathered to support a woman in labor.
11. Mayhew, *Indian Converts*, pp. 158–61.
12. At prayer many early Protestants were demonstrative and fervent. Inward feeling was accompanied by outward gesture, an act of the whole person. Warrants for praying with tears were found, for example, in Psalm 126:5, "May those who sow in tears reap with shouts of joy," and Isaiah 38:3, "And Hezekiah wept bitterly."
13. Mayhew, *Indian Converts*, pp. 244–46.

VIII

Elizabeth Bury, 1644–1720

A Pattern for Her Sex in Ages Yet Unborn

I think that looking with the heart is one of the hardest spiritual practices. I daily look at others through love and clear out snap judgments based on appearance. I began this after experiencing the pain of others' judging me. One blustery December day, I lumbered into a gift shop in winter gear. I had looked nice enough when I left home, but the clerk saw someone with a red nose and wind-blown hair. She frowned and walked away. I felt the pain of that encounter for a long time. I got to thinking about those whom I might have hurt by my glances and silent judgments and repented of it.

The Puritan Elizabeth Bury saw others through the eyes of Christ. Her extensive ministry as spiritual guide and medical practitioner took her among the poor, those to whom doctors refused treatment. She was learned in many fields, including history, mathematics, and philosophy, and was a benefactor of the persecuted and destitute, a devout soul.

Born March 2, 1644, in Clare, Suffolk, England, Elizabeth Lawrence was the second of four children born to Captain Adams Lawrence and Elizabeth Cutts. When Elizabeth was four years old, her father died. Three years later her mother married the Reverend Nathaniel Bradshaw, a faculty member of Trinity College, Cambridge University.

Elizabeth had a voracious appetite for knowledge. She learned French in order to converse with Huguenot refugees who settled in England, and studied Hebrew to understand Scripture. Her knowledge of anatomy and medicine was impressive. Religion was her favorite field and she devoted many hours to reading Scripture and theological books.

On February 1, 1667, twenty-two-year-old Elizabeth Lawrence married Griffith Lloyd, a commissioner of the peace. Their happy fifteen-year marriage ended with his death in 1682.

On March 29, 1697, she married the Reverend Samuel Bury (1663–1730), a Presbyterian minister who was a close friend of Matthew Henry and counted novelist Daniel Defoe among worshipers in his first congregation.

In 1719 Samuel received an invitation to Lewin's Mead, a Presbyterian congregation of sixteen hundred members in Bristol. Elizabeth and Samuel arrived in town April 8, 1720. On May 3 as they walked into a friend's home, Elizabeth was overcome with severe ear pain, which led to profound deafness, fever, and weakness. She died May 11, 1720.

Samuel wrote a memoir of Elizabeth based on a portion of her diary. He could not read the rest of it because she had written in shorthand for thirty years, using characters she had invented and private abbreviations.

The memoir gives us an in-depth portrait of a remarkable woman: Elizabeth was highly skilled in the practice of medicine and was sought out by the poor, in whom she perceived the presence of Christ. Her love was also expressed in a variety of charitable work: relief for persecuted refugees from France and the local poor, provision of school buildings, support of ministers and candidates for ordination who lacked government funds that were available only to Church of England members, and distribution of Bibles and other religious books to those who could not afford them.

Elizabeth funded all of this herself. Having no children, she decided to give one quarter of her income to those in need. She loved to be generous, though this was not always easy. When she was a widow, she sometimes gave away money down to the last penny because tenants were late with their payments. She observed that funds sometimes came in suddenly, "as if giving to the poor were the readiest way to bring in her debts."[1]

Elizabeth was a no-nonsense person who was disgusted by gossip and had no time for triflers. She valued time as a gift to be used in serving and glorifying God.

When not engaged in ministry, Elizabeth worshiped with others at church services, prayer assemblies, her household, or in private. She could not remember a time when she did not pray and was occasionally touched by the Holy Spirit with mystical experience that was, in her words, "beyond expression." On July 21, 1696, she wrote in her diary, "I had ravishing consolations from my Beloved that filled my heart with joy and my tongue with singing."[2]

A Pattern for Her Sex in Ages Yet Unborn

Elizabeth woke every day at 4 A.M. (5 A.M. later in life) and lifted her first thoughts to God then went to family worship[3] for Scripture reading, psalm and hymn singing, and prayer. After breakfast she retired to read Scripture along with commentary by Matthew Henry, to pray, to sing a hymn of praise, and to write in her spiritual diary.

During the day she walked with God by avoiding occasions for sin, guarding her thought and speech, lifting her soul frequently to God in prayer, and engaging in spiritual conversation with others. In the evening she prayed by herself then joined the family for prayer.

Puritans always took care to keep their devotions private, following Matthew 6:6: ". . . pray to your Father who is in secret; and your Father who sees in secret will reward you." No one heard Elizabeth pray when she was alone. But her husband, who heard her in family settings, affirmed she had a gift for prayer. He was struck with wonder at her freedom, warmth, and vigor and with the fittingness of her words. In Puritan style, she prayed with confidence and "strong expectations of blessings."

Elizabeth Bury was a loving, faith-filled woman in whom the fruits of the Spirit steadily matured. She reached out to others in spiritual concern, and they turned to her for spiritual guidance both in person and through correspondence.

Elizabeth esteemed everyone who confided in her as a child of God. She prayed for God's guidance before visiting others or writing to them and later lifted her hands to God in intercession for them.[4] Among those whom she helped were a parent whose daughter had died; someone seeking spiritual assurance; a child who wondered how to be a positive influence on her brother; an engaged woman whose judgment was clouded by greed; and a fearful friend.

Elizabeth Bury—intelligent, independent, charitable, discerning, and wise—was indeed, as Isaac Watts declared, "a pattern for her sex in ages yet unborn . . . rich in learning, yet averse to show / With charity and zeal that rarely join . . . ."[5] She cultivated the life of the mind and spirit, yoking them together to serve God and others. With a basket of medicine and prayerful heart she rode through the woods to the dejected and broken. Do we bring all that we are to bear on the hopes and needs of those to whom Christ sends us?

In the first of the following passages, Elizabeth assures a dejected person that God has not abandoned her. In the second she affirms that God doesn't make mistakes in healing us, even if God's methods and timing seem counterproductive. In the final passage, she asks God to heal the conflict in her heart.

To a Friend Under Great Dejection and Desertion

"In these dark hours of your life the silence of your friends may seem unnatural. I cannot therefore but heartily console you and beg you would not imagine your case to be unusual or out of the road of God's fatherly discipline. For what good Christian's diary did you ever read or hear of that has not such lines of complaint as yours? And no wonder, when our Head and Lord Redeemer almost dies with them in his mouth.

"Why should we grudge to pledge him in that bitter cup, whose soul was sorrowful and sore amazed? Can our jealousy argue a dereliction more than his? Are not the gifts and callings of God without repentance? If your soul has not been touched with the true loadstone, what makes it stand trembling towards its beloved point? Is not love in desire and lamenting after its object as truly love as when resting in the enjoyment? If you find much dross in your best gold, will you throw away both together? Or would you change with one who hopes without trial? . . .

"I doubt not that you address yourself to spiritual physicians, under your present maladies. Blessed be God, you have many skillful and faithful ones. Search not without their help, and may God send you a messenger, one of a thousand, who may show you your uprightness. I know that He only who creates the fruit of the lips, peace, can make your help consolatory; yet wait in the way of instituted means, and remember it was but a "little further" (Canticles 3:4) that the drowsy spouse went in search, ere she found her slighted and grieved beloved.

"I trust your present temptations to throw away your hope will not prevail. However, think not of throwing off duty, especially your attendance on that comfortable, sealing ordinance, the Lord's Supper, which I have reason to recommend to all my afflicted, tempted friends, since I find it no small mercy to go and renew my former covenant, or, if I cannot find my fidelity therein, to make it anew; for surely God doth there renew his covenant with every fallen child of Adam who heartily consents, though he cannot perfectly reach the terms [of the covenant] according to his desire. If former stated times of communicating afford you not a sufficient support, be more frequent, since every Lord's day gives you an opportunity in the city. . . .

A Pattern for Her Sex in Ages Yet Unborn

"I hope to hear you are emerging from under the waves that now overwhelm you, and by that time, you may be ready to strengthen weak hands, from more glorious appearances of God to your soul. I beg that the God of all consolation would shine on the graces he has wrought in you and will by his own methods perfect in your soul, that, when he has tried you, you may come forth as gold, and meet for the inheritance of the saints in light, where no doubt of God's love to you or of yours to him will break your peace or interrupt your joy [any]more."[6]

Healing Souls
"The all-wise Father of spirits cannot mistake in measuring, timing and appointing his methods of healing souls."[7]

The Contradictions in My Heart
"O Lord, who seest into the secret recesses of my heart, thou knowest my most ardent desires are after more holiness and resemblance to thyself. Thou gavest this thirst not to torment thy creature. Thou hast pronounced a blessing on it and promised that it shall be satisfied. But yet how little do I find my soul as yet conformed to thy image and will! Lord, shall I have the name of thy child so many years and yet no more of thy nature? O that I were more meek, merciful, humble, thankful, patient, ready to give and to forgive!

"O Lord, I have chosen thee for my portion and verily hope thou art and will be my everlasting felicity, and yet what little selfish designs and thoughts perplex my mind! I know and daily feel there is nothing in this world can satisfy my soul, and yet every little disappointment in the creature discomposes my spirit. I feel this earthly tabernacle falling and yet what little joy do I find in the prospect of my house in heaven!

"Lord, what unaccountable contradictions are there in my deceitful heart! O search and heal me!"[8]

Reflection Questions

Elizabeth perceived Christ's presence in the poor. As a spiritual exercise go to a public area, pray briefly to see others as Jesus sees them, and practice looking at others with compassion, not judgment. Reflect on this experience in your journal or discuss it with others.

Prayer was a refuge for Elizabeth. Do you feel sheltered or exposed when you pray? Explore your answer. Psalm 91 affirms that God protects those who trust divine love: "under [God's] wings you will find refuge . . ." (*4b*). When you pray, make a picture in your mind of God giving you refuge. Consider returning to this image whenever you pray.

Elizabeth guarded her thoughts and speech. We know that speaking with love and kindness matters. Why should we watch over our thoughts as well? See Hebrews 4:12. Begin being mindful of your thoughts in encounters that test your patience—when responding to others' careless driving, for example, or in similar situations.

Notes

1. Thomas Gibbons, *Memoirs of Eminently Pious Women*, abridged and supplemented by Daniel Dana (Newburyport, 1803), p. 299.
2. Elizabeth Bury, *An Account of the Life and Death of Mrs. Elizabeth Bury . . . Chiefly Collected Out of her Own Diary*, edited by Samuel Bury (Bristol, 1720), p. 137.
3. Elizabeth's "family" consisted of her husband, servants, and any guests in residence.
4. Such gestures as lifting the hands in prayer and kneeling were an essential element of Reformed devotion. For more information on the subject, see: Diane Karay Tripp, "The Reformed Tradition of Embodied Prayer," in *Liturgy: Rhythms of Prayer* 8, no. 4 (summer 1990): 91–97.
5. Isaac Watts, "An Elegy on the death of Mrs. Bury," in Gibbons, *Memoirs of Eminently Pious Women*, p. 353.
6. Gibbons, *Memoirs of Eminently Pious Women*, pp. 341–43.
7. Ibid., p. 350.
8. Ibid., pp. 329–30. September 30, 1714.

IX

Elizabeth Cairns, 1685–1741

Now I Must Walk by Starlight

When we need to know something, we can consult online tools or reference books. We can ask teachers or friends. What if you didn't have a computer, lived in an isolated rural area without library access, and had to work alone for long stretches of time? Imagine having no cell phone, radio, or television, no chummy water-cooler breaks or conversations at church. Hard to imagine, isn't it?

One child found herself alone for years with a flock of sheep and a Bible. How is it that history remembers her? She had a thirst to know things and reached out to God. God reached back and taught her. The child's name was Elizabeth Cairns.

She was born to a devout Church of Scotland couple, Covenanters, who resented the episcopal government imposed on the church by the Scottish parliament in 1661 under pressure from Charles II, and followed their ministers out of the kirks into the fields. During this period, known as the Killing Time, Covenanters were sharply persecuted. Just before her birth her parents lost their home but managed to find shelter in a small cottage just in time, and a minister baptized Elizabeth during the night.

Elizabeth began working as a shepherd when she was five or six years old and helped her father with farm chores. She was lonely and regretted not attending school or church services. She learned to read when she was about seven, carried a Bible with her to the fields, and read as the sheep grazed.

The Scripture seemed to shimmer with light. Elizabeth began to discern between good and evil, recognized she was a sinner, and began to realize that Christ was her Savior. When she turned ten, God began to illumine her understanding by highlighting certain passages with power. At other times God withdrew, which helped her grow in spiritual maturity. Sometimes she was so absorbed in meditation and prayer that she forgot to look after the sheep but never lost one.

While Elizabeth was young, the whole region suffered a seven-year famine. Often the only food she had consisted of scraps a neighbor's daughter shared as they watched sheep together.

When she was about twenty-two years old, she enrolled in a three-month course to train as a seamstress and moved in with a family in Stirling, the town where she would live most of the rest of her life. After a while she returned home, but found it impossible to live with her parents. She returned to Stirling and began working as a domestic servant. When she was thirty-six her ailing parents came to live with her. Elizabeth commented, "I . . . thought it my duty to wait on them in their old age, and as a part of my generation work I had to do in the world . . . ."[1]

When her father died a few months later, Elizabeth and her mother moved into quarters near the kirk. She now ran a thriving school but worried about her mother, who was in great pain. "Many a time," Elizabeth noted, "I was forced to run out of hearing and stop my ears, the extremity of her trouble was so great. O! I can neither word nor write the extremity I underwent between my own case and her affliction."[2] Until this point Elizabeth had written in her journal. Now she stopped and did not resume writing until four years later. She carried on teaching and caring for her bedfast mother. Another trial befell them when a relative robbed them of almost everything they owned. After nine years of illness Elizabeth's mother died.

Elizabeth doesn't disclose much more about her life after this. A few weeks before her death, she left her Stirling home to visit friends in Edinburgh. She fell ill at Leith and died there April 4, 1741.

Let's consider Elizabeth's spiritual life. John Greig, who edited her memoir, writes that she did not experience sudden conversion "like a mushroom that comes up in a night," but was one in whom the seed of baptismal grace was planted and steadily grew, having fallen on good soil.[3]

By age fourteen, Elizabeth claimed spirituality as her element. "God being my all . . . I knew not how to live without him."[4] She was clearly a mystic: from the ages of fourteen to eighteen she was graced with frequent spiritual insight and was often visited by the divine presence as she prayed or partook of the Lord's Supper:

"One night in secret prayer I was so raised in my soul that in some measure I may say, whether in the body or out of the body I cannot tell, but this I do remember, I was turned to behold the glory from which there shined a light unto my soul that strengthened and capacitated it to behold glorious objects and unexpressible mysteries . . . and here I was allowed, as it were, to come near God . . . ."[5]

Another day she recalled sitting down with her Bible, praying for a blessing on her reading:

". . . Immediately there shined a light in my soul that represented to my view those glorious mysteries that so transported me, that I could read none, but turned over the leaves and beheld the glory that shined in it: so I laid by my Bible and fell to prayer and praise . . . ."[6]

One Sunday morning the Presence drew near her as she sat at the communion table:

"At the table there shone a light on my soul that so transported me that I dare not take upon me to mark down what I was allowed to behold; but this I can say, I was allowed in my meditation to travel, as it were, between the cross and the crown, there I considered Mount Calvary and what was done there, and through those elements of bread and wine, I got a distinct view of the sufferings of Christ, and also to me this was a Mount Pisgah, where I got a view of the promised land, in faith of being possessed of it after death."[7]

Reflecting on this joyful period, Elizabeth wrote, "I can say from my own experience that in one half hour's real and sensible communion with God there is more joy, more pleasure, and unexpressible advantage than all the pleasures of youth and profits that ever the world could afford me."[8]

One afternoon in her nineteenth year, Elizabeth was meditating when a thought surfaced:

"What ground hast thou for those comfortable hopes and expectations that thou hast entertained the last year?"[9] She was fearful and confused and did not move for two hours. Thus began a seven-year "dark cloud of desertion"[10] in which she struggled with spiritual aridity, doubt, and temptation.

She found no help when she turned to ministers and others for counsel. Eventually she realized she was helpless to relieve her own suffering; only God could heal her soul.

Elizabeth appears to have endured a "night of sense" and a "night of the spirit," traditional terms for long periods in which God cleanses a soul from self-centeredness. During the night of sense she lived without "sensible down-pourings of the Spirit" she previously enjoyed. As the night of the spirit took hold, her sense of desolation intensified. She felt "deadness and powerlessness overspread [her] soul." What is the "deadness" to which she referred? It is the spiritual process that Scripture likens to a grain of wheat dying to bear much fruit (*John 12:24*). Even as Elizabeth mourned the absence of spiritual consolations, she realized she was maturing in faith, hope, patience, and humility and began to sense God's presence in a way she could not put into words.

One day while she was praying she felt the light return and was "sweetly transported." Her love for God was so strong it burned like a flame. She had an intense sense of God's presence for a month, then found herself "stripped of enjoyments" again.

When she least expected it, God drew aside the veil clouding her soul and filled her with such love that she felt struck down as dead while her soul was lifted high.

For the rest of her life—as she cared for her ailing parents, taught, and endured various trials—Elizabeth occasionally had a strong sense of God's presence, followed by long periods of everyday quiet. "Now I must walk by starlight," she wrote.[11] She trusted and prayed when God seemed absent. She also grew ever more certain of a truth that God had taught her as a child: light shines in darkness and is never overcome. May we take heart from Elizabeth when we face our own starlit path and come to know God's presence by God's comings and goings.

The following passages are taken from Elizabeth's spiritual memoir and provide rare glimpses into the life of a Reformed mystic. Follow her as she comes to understand how the Spirit can illumine the soul, learns to grow from spiritual infancy to adulthood, and places herself unconditionally in God's hands.

There Shined a Light into My Soul

"It was my employment for several years to keep my father's cattle. From the eighth to the tenth year of my age I was much delighted with my book [Bible], so that I was not only content with the reading of it, but so retained it on my mind that when I had not time to read, I might have it to meditate on. All the daytime, I was still in the fields alone with my flock; but in the winter seasons, especially in the long nights, I was busy getting lessons from any that would teach me, and whenever I could read distinctly by myself, I carried my book always with me, and as I read, there shined a light on my mind, so that I was filled with wonder at everything I read.

"From the tenth to the sixteenth year of my life, it pleased God in holy sovereign grace and mercy to [disclose] both my misery and the remedy more clearly . . . . For in the former two years, wherein I was filled with wonder, the word was all alike to me, but now there were passages sent into my mind with power suitable to my case.

"I remember one day I went to pray, as I was wont to do, and that word was brought into my mind, Proverbs 15:8, 'The sacrifice of the wicked is an abomination to the Lord.' On which I fell a thinking and applied it to myself, and I saw that although my conscience could not charge me with a wicked life, yet I had a wicked nature, and by this I came to see that although I had never committed actual sin, yet there was as much sin in my nature as would make my best duties hateful to God, and so I went to prayer again, with these words in my mouth, Oh! That God would renew me after his own image and give to me his Spirit and enlighten my mind in the saving knowledge of himself, and that Scripture was brought to my mind, Hosea 6:3: 'Then shall we know, if we follow on to know the Lord,' etc. and Proverbs 8:17: 'And they that seek me early shall find me.'

"After this I felt more light and power in reading the word and was taught to observe the inward frame of my heart. At this time the particular places of the word of God I was most delighted with were the four evangelists. O how pleasant was it to me to read over the birth, life, and death of the blessed Redeemer! As also the book of psalms, many of which I retained on my mind and sang them when I was alone. There was also the Song of Solomon and the prophecy of Isaiah.

"And it being my lot to live alone, and none to instruct me in what I read, and having no opportunity of hearing the gospel preached because of my employment, so when I read those Scriptures, I fell a reasoning what this and the other expression meant, and therewith I went to God and plead with him by prayer that he might open mine eyes that I might sees the wonders of his law.

"After this there shined a light into my soul by which the word was made a lamp unto my feet and a light to my paths, insomuch that there was no action, either religious, moral, or natural, but that this light [revealed] the law to be a rule to them. But this light did not always continue, and so I came to know it by its comings and goings. I observed that when it was absent, my prayers were so many dead words, and the word itself a dead letter. But when this light was present, my prayers went well with me. . . ."[12]

She Lets the Child Walk Alone

"I was pleading with God in prayer that he would remove the darkness from my soul and lift on me the light of his countenance again. And as I continued pleading, my soul was like to turn desperate, and I opened my mouth thus unreasonably to God and said, 'Take away my life [before] thou take away the light of thy countenance,' and immediately the veil was drawn aside and I got a sight of his glory. But O this pleasant blink lasted but for a moment, and my darkness did immediately return.

"And on the day following, that word was brought to me with power, Psalm 31:15, 'My times are wholly in thy hand.' This I applied to myself and said, My times are also wholly in God's hand, and I believe he will order them for my good. So I went on for several days pleading and hoping that my enjoyments would return again, but alas! I was disappointed.

"After this there was one who was reported [to be] an experienced Christian, with whom I endeavored to be acquaint[ed]. And after converse with her, I imparted some of my mind to her and told her of my sweet life I had enjoyed through the last year and what a sudden deprival I had met with.

"She told me that I must part with that life or I must go out of the world, as also she told me of a life of faith a believer lived by in this world, and that sensible manifestations were reserved for eternity.

"And by a similitude she taught me that Christ did with his young converts as a woman doth with her child. When it is young, she carries it in her arms and leads it by the hands. But when it comes to more strength, she lets it walk alone and take a fall and rise again, and yet her love is still the same. So doth Christ with his people in their first entry into his way. He manifests much of his love to them, but when they come to more experience, he withdraws sense from them, that they may be taught to walk by faith. But yet his love [for them] is still the same.

"As also she told me that I must not think always to enjoy the blinks of divine light and love, but I must come down from the mount of manifestations and take part of the dark steps of the wilderness, as the cloud of witnesses that had gone before me had done."[13]

Here I Am; Send Me

"One day as I was in prayer, it pleased a sovereign and gracious God, as it were, to rend the veil, where I met with a renewed discovery of glorious Christ in the sweet rays of his glory and manifestations of his divine love that ravished me and brought me near hand, and so filled me with a sense of his love that I could hold no more.

"So I remained as if I had been in possession for some time, but what I here both felt and saw, I will neither word nor write, and so the veil returned and covered the manifested glory I then beheld. And when I saw the light of this world again, I earnestly desired to be dissolved, that so I might win to behold the bright and glorious face of my Redeemer, and swim in his infinite fullness to all eternity.

"And while I was thus breathing after perfection, that word Isaiah 6:8, 'Here I am; send me,' came with such power and rebuke that I immediately applied it to myself, and thought it was my duty to say with the prophet, 'Here am I; send me,' about whatever the Lord had yet to do with me in this world, either in the way of duty or yet in the way of suffering; it was still my duty to be at his call."[14]

Reflection Questions

Elizabeth endured a seven-year "cloud of desertion," when she received no spiritual comfort. What spiritual fruits might result from the dark night? Can you think of a Scripture reference? Thomas Keating suggests Lazarus of Bethany as a paradigm for transformation.[15]

Elizabeth says that when light shined in her soul she could pray, but the absence of the light undermined prayerfulness. Paul affirms that the Holy Spirit helps us to pray (*Rom. 8:26–27*). Can we pray without the Holy Spirit?

"Here I am; send me," says the prophet Isaiah (*6:8*). Consider praying these words as Elizabeth did, to be available to God.

Notes

1. Elizabeth Cairns, *Memoirs of the Life of Elizabeth Cairns, Written By Herself some Years before her Death*, edited by John Greig (Glasgow, 1762), p.130.
2. Ibid., p. 140.
3. Ibid., Preface to the Reader, pp. viii, ix.
4. Ibid., p. 23.
5. Ibid, p. 31.
6. Ibid., pp. 35–36.
7. Ibid., p. 36.
8. Ibid., p. 43.
9. Ibid., p. 45.
10. Ibid., p. 45. This is Elizabeth's term.
11. Ibid., p. 112.
12. Ibid., pp. 15–17.
13. Ibid., pp. 46–47.
14. Ibid., p. 80.
15. John 11:1–44; *The Better Part* (New York: Continuum, 2000), pp. 20–26.

X

Deborah Prince, 1723–1744

Implacable

Doubt is a normal part of the Christian life. Even the disciples doubted when faced with the risen Jesus (*Luke 24:41*). Occasionally people carry doubt to extremes. What does this look like? Consider a young woman who lived at the center of the first great religious revival in North America and rejected her conversion experience.

Deborah Prince was a studious young woman born to Deborah Denny, an English immigrant, and Thomas Prince (1687–1758), pastor of Old South [Congregational] Church, Boston, one of the most respected ministers of his generation. Since Deborah burned most of her writings when she was depressed, we must rely on him to tell her story.

She was raised in a home that valued piety and intellect. Leading theologians of the day, such as Jonathan Edwards and George Whitefield, gathered at the Prince home, and Deborah probably listened to their discussions and may have participated in them. She studied the Bible and religious and historical works.

When Deborah turned fourteen, she was ready to join the church and to receive the Lord's Supper. At the last moment she felt unworthy and refrained from approaching the table. It took a near-death experience to lead her back.

On July 18, 1739, when Deborah was fifteen, she and her father started on a boat trip to visit her uncle. They stood on a small boat drawn next to a larger vessel. Thomas reached out to help her board the ship, but suddenly the little boat veered and both of them fell overboard and sank out of sight. Deborah's sister and brother looked on helplessly for a minute, then several strangers dove in and pulled father and daughter to safety. A month later, Deborah joined the Old South Church.

Trusted Voices

By 1740 the Great Awakening[1] was sweeping through New England. Deborah was beginning to doubt her previous spiritual experience and feared she had not received Christ into her heart. On December 13, 1740, she had a conversion experience while reading the story of Jesus healing the leper.[2] Her father remarked that "there came into her such a sweet and raised view both of the power, willingness and will of this dear Redeemer to cleanse her from the leprosy of sin and save her, as to satisfy her of it, and draw her to him in such a manner as she never felt before."[3]

Neither Thomas Prince, Deborah's father, nor Joseph Sewell, his colleague at Old South Church, would ever fully understand the next turn in Deborah's spiritual journey.

She began attending the revival meetings of the Presbyterian fireball Gilbert Tennent (1702–1764). At that time, Tennent preached the wrath of God and dissected human behavior and intention under a microscope. Deborah took him at his word and began to fear she was spiritually deceived. Every doubt led her to examine her soul and to conclude that she was deluded.

Her father looked on sadly. "I think," he said thoughtfully, "she should have humbly received every comfort which the sovereign God by the Scriptures offered her . . . ."[4]

In Tennent's published sermons we can see what led Deborah to label herself a deluded sinner. In 1735 Tennent asserted that most people "securely sleep in sin and betray themselves into irreparable and endless ruin by vain and presumptuous hopes of mercy." He hoped to expose "the numerous dangers of such fatal delusions and destructive mistakes."[5] Addressing presumptuous souls who erroneously claimed to be saved, Tennent exclaimed, "O sinner! Think how horrible will thy case be when all that is in God will be stirred up against thee . . . . "[6] and more to the point: "Look here yon bold rebel, here is the glittering brandishing sword of the terrible God held before thee, which, if thou turn not speedily, shall stab thee through with eternal death."[7] True penitents, he warned, must loathe sin: "Thy hatred must be universal and implacacle . . . ."[8]

Deborah Prince became implacable. On May 29, 1744, she fell ill with a fever and berated herself, complaining of "hardness of heart, blindness of mind, impenitence and unbelief . . . ."[9] She denied having experienced sanctifying grace and believed that her previous experiences of spiritual comfort were delusional. Thomas first realized that his daughter was very ill on July 1; at the same time,

Implacable

Deborah sensed that she would not survive her illness and agonized, feeling unprepared to meet her Judge and Redeemer. Her father listened to her cries, and his heart broke: ". . . the horror of that night! It was one of the most distressing I ever knew!"[10]

As Deborah's darkness continued, Thomas tried to reason with her. But she lamented, "You don't know what a vile creature I am; I have dreadfully apostatized from Christ . . . ."[11] She begged him to pray for her as an unconverted sinner. Thomas did as his daughter asked, but didn't stop speaking to her of Christ's compassion or attempting to comfort her with Scripture. Deborah remained implacable. Rev. Sewell also visited without success. "We found that none but the Almighty himself could do it," her father concluded.[12] Both pastors believed she was a child of God but since she did not feel the comfort of the Spirit, they had no choice but to leave her in darkness and to pray for her.

Deborah continued without light until July 20, near sunset, about half an hour before her death. Around six o'clock her physician told her he could do nothing more, and Thomas told his daughter it was time for him to commend her into God's care.

Suddenly Deborah became calm. After a few minutes she opened her eyes and, though weak, began to whisper, "O I love the Lord Jesus with all my heart! I see such an amiableness, such an amiableness in him! I prize him above a thousand worlds!" Asked if she could now entrust herself to her Savior, she replied, "O yes, I believe in him! I rejoice in him! And I rejoice in all the agonies I have borne!"[13]

Full of joy, she continued whispering with messages for others: "Tell . . . all the society, for the strengthening of their faith and their encouragement to go on! Tell [A.] not to mind the vanities of the world, but to seek to make her hope stronger. . . . Tell [B.] not to be so careful about worldly matters but to be more careful about Christ and grace. . . ."[14] After several more messages, Thomas perceived that she was slipping away.

"Lord Jesus, receive my spirit," she breathed, then died without a sound while her family and friends prayed at her side.[15]

Was Deborah Prince a deluded sinner until her deathbed experience? Joseph Sewell and Thomas Prince, two pastors trusted by hundreds of people, didn't think so. Is it possible that sermons urging total mistrust of the Spirit's grace were damaging to her spirit? Yes. Could Deborah have misinterpreted her experience? Yes. Since her father noted that she was once depressed, we should be aware that serious spiritual problems might have underlying medical and/or emotional causes or interactions.[16] May her ordeal remind us of the importance of spiritual discernment, reassure us of the faithfulness of God, and caution us to take all factors into account before leaping to purely religious conclusions about our well-being.

One of Deborah's few surviving writings is her plan for daily worship. It includes most of the elements of traditional Reformed devotional practice. Note that even as she prayed "in secret," following Jesus' guidance in Matthew 6:6, she brought others into her circle of prayer by praying for them and asked God to guide her interactions with others. A faithful Christian's prayer may be private, but it is never simply personal. Even our requests for individual blessing will have important consequences for others, for as one Puritan writer paraphrased Cyprian, the early church writer, "We pray not for one, but for the whole church, because we are all one."[17]

The Method I Intend by God's Grace to Keep Every Day
"In the Morning

"Rise at five.

"As soon as I am dressed, endeavor to praise God for his mercies the night past, and beg his assistance in reading his most holy word.

"Then read some portion of Scripture and meditate upon it, or read some expositor upon it.

"Then address myself to God upon my knees: adore and praise him for all his goodness to me, confess my sins and utter unworthiness of the least of his mercies, beg for the pardon of them in and through Christ, and for grace and help against them in the time to come, and to resist and overcome all the temptations of the day. Beg for the presence of God with me throughout the day, enabling me to do the duties of it, and guiding me in all the affairs of it, enabling me to do all to his glory.

"Then set myself about my lawful business, endeavoring all the day to keep a strict watch over my thoughts, words and actions.

"At Noon

"About twelve o'clock, if I can, retire to praise God for his goodness to the whole world of mankind, and to recommend them to him for his particular favor. Remember and intercede for friends and relations in a particular manner.

"Then read a chapter [of the Bible].

"At Night

"Retire into my chamber as soon as possible, and first, examine how I have spent the day: what mercies I have enjoyed, what sins I have committed, and what duties I have omitted.

"Then address myself to God through Christ for pardon, peace and cleansing, returning humble and hearty thanks for the mercies of the day past, and conclude with committing my soul and body into his hands.

"Read a portion of holy Scripture, and if it is pretty seasonable, some other good book, and so go to sleep."[18]

Reflection Questions

What is the distinction between soul-searching confession and self-disparagement? The liturgies of Reformed churches remind us that God in Christ has already forgiven us. Consider the Call to Confession that begins, "The proof of God's amazing love is this: While we were yet sinners, Christ died for us. Let us therefore approach the throne of grace with boldness."[19]

Why does worship frame the prayer of confession with a reminder of God's kindness to us in Christ in the call to confession and the declaration of pardon?

What danger is there in trusting only our feelings? Why?

Trusted Voices

People isolated from Christian community sometimes develop unsound religious ideas. What are the benefits of regular public worship? of the varied menu of Scripture provided in the lectionary? of in-depth interaction with other Christians?

Deborah Prince made a habit of regularly interceding for others when she prayed at midday. When Jesus prayed for his disciples, he prayed for them because they belonged to God, not for any other reason (*John 17:9*). How might it change us to pray for others, realizing that they are beloved daughters and sons of God?

Notes

1. "Great Awakening": a term applied to a widespread revival in the United States that reached a high point in New England in the early 1740s with the preaching of George Whitefield and Jonathan Edwards. Deborah, therefore, lived at its epicenter.
2. Luke 5:12–16.
3. [Thomas Prince,] *The Sovereign God Acknowledged and Blessed . . . A Sermon Occasioned by the Decease of [Mistress] Deborah Prince* (Boston, 1744), p. 23.
4. Ibid., p. 24.
5. Gilbert Tennent, *Solemn Warning to the Secure World . . . The Presumptuous Sinner Detected . . .* (Boston, 1735), p. 1.
6. Ibid., p. 5.
7. Ibid., p. 7.
8. Ibid., p. 20.
9. Prince, *Sovereign God*, p. 25.
10. Ibid., p. 26.
11. Ibid.
12. Ibid., p. 28.
13. Ibid., p. 31.
14. Ibid.
15. Prince, *Sovereign God*, p. 32.
16. Deborah may have suffered "scrupulosity," a form of obsessive-compulsive disorder, in which a person has an overzealous concern that her thoughts or behavior displeases God. See: www.ocdonline.com article "God Forbid" by Steven Phillipson, Ph.D.
17. William Gouge, *A Guide to Goe to God* (London, 1626), p. 21, freely quoting from Cyprian, *De Oratione Dominica* (ch. ii).
18. Deborah Prince, "Appendix, Containing Copies of some of her Papers," in Prince, *Sovereign God*, pp. 37–38.
19. *The Worship Sourcebook* (Grand Rapids: CRC Publications, 2004), pp. 82, 83. See also Presbyterian Church (U.S.A.) and the Cumberland Presbyterian Church, *Book of Common Worship* (Louisville, KY: Westminster/John Knox Press, 1993), p. 52, no. 2.

XI

Temperance Hannibal, fl. c. 1754

I Heard a Voice Saying, "Follow Me"

I was nineteen years old, relaxing on my bed. Suddenly my attention was abruptly focused on an inner vision: I was falling, plunging through dark emptiness for what seemed like miles. I wondered what was at the bottom or if there was a bottom at all and was filled with dread. Suddenly, I was caught in a comforting net. I rested and saw sunlight streaming through the window. I knew that I was helpless to help myself; I knew that I owed my rescue to God and needed to depend on God always.

I felt a shock of recognition when I read the vision of a woman who lived two hundred years before I was born. As you read her story, consider the mysterious ways that God has reached out to you. Fathomless grace is strange but true.

The Mohegan Presbyterian missionary Samson Occom took a reservation census of the Montaukett Indians of Long Island, New York, in 1760 and recorded one hundred and sixty-two people, six of whom were surnamed Hannibal. Temperance was probably one of them. Occom recorded her spiritual-awakening testimony in a diary detailing his work among her people. It is the only information we have about Temperance and the only such Montaukett statement that exists.

Thanks to Occom, we know a little about her religious life. The community gathered for Sunday worship around 10 A.M. Occom read a psalm or hymn of Isaac Watts and explored its meaning, then the congregation sang it. Prayer followed, with more singing and a portion of Scripture. Occom preached a brief sermon then concluded the service with more prayer and psalm singing. The people worshiped on Sunday afternoon and evening in the same manner and also worshiped together on Wednesday evenings.[1]

Trusted Voices

Samson Occom persuaded many Long Island and other New England Native Americans to move away from European-American colonists to prevent cultural erosion and corrupting influences. One migration was attempted in 1775–76 but failed due to the beginning of the Revolutionary War. The second migration occurred in 1785–86. The Hannibal family did not leave but survived well into the nineteenth century.[2]

Occom observed that the Native Americans found joy in singing psalms, hymns, and spiritual songs. They sang as they worked, husking corn, for example, and also sang together in the evening.

One October Monday in 1785 he drew near a house and heard "melodious singing." "We went in amongst them," he wrote in his diary, "and they all took hold of my hand one by one with joy and gladness from the greatest to the least, and we sot down a while and then they began to sing again . . . ."[3] Temperance probably found joy in singing psalms to God.

She is one of those whose life is largely hidden from our view, yet it was a life hidden with Christ. In her vision she found the One who is able to keep us from falling.[4] Our lives are also hidden in Christ. Future generations may find few traces of our existence too, yet our value is known to our Creator, who has written our name on the palm of his hand: "I will not forget you."[5]

Here is the full text of Temperance Hannibal's conversion account. It gives us a moving glimpse of one woman's encounter with Christ and the safety she found in accepting his invitation, Follow me.

Spiritual-Awakening Narrative
February 7, 1754?

I have been the most wi[**] wretch that ever live, yea [ ], there was nothing in all the Nois of Religion, and I thought and Said that the Christians Lied; I thought it was best for me to gratify my own Inclinations—Till the Last fall, I was Sick for Some Time, and in my Sickness, I began to Query what wo[ ] become of my Soul, if I shoud Die in this State and Condition, and these thoughts threw me into Fright, and was Concern'd for my Soul for Some Time, but as I got well of my Sickness my Concern wore a way ____ ____ till this Late Religious Stir I bethought of my Self aga[ ] and after I had been to few Meetings I found my Self a great Sinner, and an undone Creature before god, yea Saw my

I Heard a Voice Saying, "Follow Me"

Self fit for nothing but Hell and everlasting Distruction _____ and as I was at one meeting and as I was amusing and Considering my State & Condition, it threw me into Such Horror and guil of Concionce and Confusion of face, I fell into a Swaun, and immediately I found my Self into great Darkness, and While I was there I heard a voice before me, Saying follow me, and I went that way, and Immediately found my Self upon Something I cant Compared to nothing but a Pole [crossed out: but over] Put over a deep hole.[6]

Reflection Questions

Have you ever felt, like Temperance, that religion was irrelevant? What changed your views?

Temperance had a visionary experience of Christ. What touchstone do we have to discern whether such an experience derives from God or is a deception of the Adversary?

Temperance was one whose life was hidden with Christ. Did Jesus have a special ministry to hidden people with little status? Think of some examples. Who might Jesus befriend if he were in your shoes? How can you befriend them?

Notes

1. Samson Occom, "Sam Occum's Diary, 1744–1790," ed. Julia Clark in Gaynell Stone, ed., *The History & Archaeology of the Montauk*, Readings in Long Island Archaeology & Ethnohistory, vol. 3., 2nd ed. (Stony Brook, N.Y.: Suffolk County Archaeological Association, 1993), pp. 239–40.
2. Philip Rabito-Wyppensenwah, "The Hannibals: A Montaukett Family History," in Stone, ed., *History & Archaeology of the Montauk*, pp. 350ff.
3. Occom, "Sam Occum's Diary," in Stone, ed., *History & Archaeology of the Montauk*, p. 248.
4. Jude 24.
5. Isaiah 49:15c.
6. Occom, "Sam Occum's Diary," p. 232.

XII

Mary Hutson, d. 1757

I Laid the Bible to My Heart

People seem to have a terrible time embracing humility. Why else would Jesus have talked about it so much? He had only to glance at his disciples to see self-centered people fighting for first place.[1] Benjamin Franklin spoke for us when he declared: "Even if I could conceive that I had completely overcome [my pride], I should probably be proud of my humility."[2] Jesus suggested that his followers emulate a child. We can also look to an adult who embodied humility, the sure path to God's presence.

Mary Hutson was praised as a shining example for other Christians. She was either English or American and married William Hutson, a New York actor who emigrated from England after rejecting the legal profession. He was converted during one of George Whitefield's New York revivals then traveled south and began teaching slaves in a school sponsored by the Huspah Chapel, about twenty miles from Beaufort, [South] Carolina.

In 1743 William was ordained as pastor of the chapel, later named Stoney Creek Independent Presbyterian Church. Mary joined the congregation July 22, 1743.

She bore seven children between 1744 and 1755, of whom six survived infancy.[3] The family depended on slave labor to free them from many domestic responsibilities. In 1756 they settled in Charleston, where William became one of the pastors of the Congregational church founded around 1690. Mary fell ill and died in November 1757; William lived four more years.

Spirituality permeated Mary's life. Several times a day she withdrew to a quiet place for prayer, meditation, and self-examination. The whole family probably worshiped together each morning and evening and attended church services on the Lord's Day. In Puritan fashion she performed ordinary actions prayerfully. One Sunday after her private prayer she wrote in her diary, "I am now going to cleanse the body that I may appear decently in the house of God: O! that Jesus would cleanse my soul . . . ."[4]

One April morning Mary read from the last chapter of Hosea [14:8b–c]: "It is I who answer and look after you. I am like an evergreen cypress; your faithfulness comes from me." She closed the book. Then, in her own words, "I opened the Bible and laid it to my heart, with those words (which I have often used at school without thought): 'My book and heart shall never part.' "[5]

Like Dorothy Leigh, Mary Hutson accepted the call to spiritual motherhood. She sought to embody the Christ-centeredness she hoped to nurture in her children. Mary's children probably observed her praying at mealtime, laying the Bible to her bosom, and reverently attending to small tasks in the presence of the Lord. Do we embody our belief? Can others read mercy in our eyes? Do they sense the presence of the Other who looks after and loves all?

The following is a portion of an advice letter Mary wrote to her children. In the letter, she encourages them to be faithful, merciful, humble, and just. Note how she connects God's glory, the welfare of others, and peace of heart. Following this excerpt are two prayers in which we see Mary's desire for spiritual progress.

Spiritual Advice to Her Children
"My Dearest Children,
Whilst you are reading these lines, your poor mama's hands that wrote them, her tongue that entreated you to come to Christ and prayed over you, and her eyes that have often wept over you, and her heart that has been poured out to God with strong cries for your perishing souls, I say these will be moldering in the cold grave, the house appointed for all living. And what, shall all my endeavors be lost? And all the instructions you have had from your tender pious father? All the good examples he has set before you; all the excellent sermons you have heard from him and other faithful ministers, shall all, I say, be lost? Or, which is worse, rise up in the judgment against you? God forbid!

"O my children! How could I weep over you, were it possible, with tears of blood. I pray you, I entreat you, by the mercies of God, by the agony and bloody sweat of Christ, by his cross and passion, by his precious death and burial, by his resurrection and glorious ascension, and by the coming of the Holy Ghost, I charge you, be ye reconciled to God. How do I travail again in birth with you, till Christ be formed in you! As an evidence of my tender concern for you, I leave this behind me, that by it, when [I am] dead, I may yet speak to you. . . .

"I charge you, as you name the name of Christ, to depart from all iniquity. Fly from the very appearance of sin. Shun evil company, lest you should be found partakers of their sins and infected with their ways. Associate yourselves with the excellent ones of the earth, real Christians.

"Strive, if possible, to sit under a sound faithful minister. Search the Scriptures; read a chapter or two every day; prize them above the choicest gold, so shall they become sweeter to you than honey or the honeycomb; blessed be God I find them so.

"Read none but good books. Be sure to pray in secret morning and evening. If you have it in your power, choose that business or calling which will be most for the glory of God, the good of your souls, and the benefit of others, which are all connected together. In a few words, *do justice, love mercy, and walk humbly with God.*[6]

"And again, I would entreat you to strive against pride. Don't despise the poor, for of such is the kingdom of heaven. Pray hard for humility and pray for that faith which purifies the soul and works by love. Pray that you may love God with all your heart, mind, and strength. Love your brothers and sisters. Love all your Christian brethren and love your enemies.

"Feed the hungry, clothe the naked, visit the sick, and whatever else is necessary, ask of God and he will teach you, so shall you have grace here and peace, such peace as the world can never give nor take away, even that peace of God which passes all understanding, and hereafter you shall have an eternal weight of glory, which God grant for Christ's sake.

"Adieu, my dear children, till we meet, I hope, in glory.
Mary Hutson"[7]

Better Fruit for the Future
"Lord Jesus! I pray thee to clothe me with humility and make me thankful. May I be more diligent and fruitful in every good word and work than I have been in times past!"[8]

"Lord, I pray thee, for Christ's sake, grant that the word I have heard this day may sink deep into my heart, so that I may bring forth better fruit for the future than I have done yet."[9]

Reflection Questions
Parents often give their children advice, but how much spiritual guidance do children receive? Make a point to offer children loving words of encouragement.

In discussing vocational choices, Mary states that glorifying God is connected to the welfare of one's soul and the welfare of others. Why does she say this? Can you think of Scripture passages to support this idea?

Mary encourages her children to "ask of God and he will teach you." Do you find it natural to turn to God for guidance? Read Matthew 7:7–11 and Philippians 4:6. Take these words to heart.

Notes
1. Mark 9:34; Luke 22:24.
2. Benjamin Franklin, *The Works of Benjamin Franklin*, ed. John Bigelow, vol. 1 (New York: G. P. Putnam's Sons, 1904), p. 203.
3. William Hutson, "Register," in *The South Carolina Historical and Genealogical Magazine* 38 (1937): 21–36. The children's names and dates of baptism (or burial): Mary (December 30, 1744); Elizabeth (June 8, 1746); William (March 19, 1749); Thomas (February 27, 1751); Esther (April 21, 1753); William (buried October 26, 1754); Anne (February 22, 1755).
4. Mary Hutson, "Living Christianity Delineated in the Diary and Letters of Mrs. Mary Hutson, of South Carolina," in Hugh Bryan and Mary Hutson, *Living Christianity Delineated* (London, 1760), p. 142.
5. Ibid., p. 135.
6. Cf. Micah 6:8. Italics are in the original.
7. Hutson, "Living Christianity," pp. 154–55, 157–58.
8. Ibid., p. 134.
9. Ibid., p. 144.

XIII

Mary Somervel, c. 1678–1762

My Soul Was Ravished Within Me

Indiana is fairly plain as states go. It has no oceans, mountains, or breathtaking scenery. Notre Dame quarterbacks speeding toward goalposts don't count as natural wonders. Sometimes we can't get from Point A to Point B fast enough. Hence another name for U.S. Highway 31 connecting north and south: state drag strip. But there is much beauty if you get out of the car, walk, and slow your eye. My late friend Stan once mused that because the Midwest has no arresting landscapes, we are forced to turn inward and create beauty.

Perhaps deprivation does encourage us to cultivate the inner life. The story of one Scottish child seems to bear this out.

One morning five-year-old Mary was famished and fixed her eyes on the steaming food on the table. She was not allowed to eat until her family first prayed and sang. As she joined in the psalm, God flooded her with sweetness and joy and she was not hungry the rest of the day.

In middle age, the Spirit whispered to Mary repeatedly, "Make known my name unto my brethren by declaring what I have done for thee."[1] She complied. Her narrative, *The Spiritual Experiences of Mary Somervel,* originally written to encourage her nieces and nephews, was published a few years after her death.

Mary Somervel was born in Ayrshire, Scotland, around 1678 to two Covenanters, those within the Church of Scotland who clung to Presbyterian worship when the Scottish parliament imposed episcopal polity and worship in 1661. Her parents were among those harassed and persecuted. Though many of Covenanter persuasion later broke away from the established church to form the Associate Presbytery (later known as the Associate Synod), Mary never left the Church of Scotland.

Trusted Voices

When her father died, her mother and the five children were evicted from the family farm and pursued through the mountains by government soldiers. Covenanters were hunted down because they refused to recognize King Charles II as head of the church, defied his legal authority, and refused to submit to church oversight by bishops. A few years after the death of Mary's father, her mother died. Orphaned at age ten, Mary began working as a servant for a family in the town of Ayr. She remained a domestic servant for the rest of her life and lived in a simple cottage. Not much else is known of her daily life except that she learned to read and write and suffered from frailty and illness.

Mary Somervel was a mystic who received the inflowing of God's presence and touches of divine grace. Her first mystical experience was the sudden stilling of her appetite when she was five years old. When she was ten years old, the same year that she was orphaned, God consoled her by so filling her senses and soul with light and love that she was lost in "ravishment and ecstasy."

During an evening worship service in 1719, Mary was so "brimful of the consolations of God" that she longed to retire to a quiet place. After the benediction, she headed for the woods near the kirk and began to pray while darkness overtook her. Having assurance from God that she would be safe, she prayed for several hours among the trees, swallowed up in God's presence.

Some time later, Mary contracted a stomach ailment. After three years she concluded that only death could relieve her pain. One day a physician came, pronounced her condition dangerous, and said he had no medicine to give her. She asked him to pray, believing that only God could heal her. Later another doctor came and prayed. Around midnight Mary heard God say, "The sun of righteousness will arise with healing in his wings,"[2] and she felt an unseen tender hand spread a covering over her pain while the voice continued to whisper in her ear. One minute she was in such pain that she could not shift her position in bed, and the next she was pain-free and spiritually refreshed. The ailment never returned. "From sweet experience I can say, my God is my physician . . . how can I but give praises to him?"[3]

Though sometimes graced by extraordinary evidence of God's closeness, Mary did not live in continual awareness of the divine presence. She occasionally wondered if she was a child of God or a hypocrite and experienced desert times in prayer and extraordinary spiritual dejection.

My Soul Was Ravished Within Me

In 1729, when Mary was about fifty years old, God overpowered her in ecstasy once more. "My soul was ravished within me, so that I cried out . . . my love was enflamed . . . there were . . . showers of blessings poured down, and my soul was so filled with a sense of the love of God and the consolations of the Holy Ghost, as made me cry out, 'O Lord, I am but a clay vessel. Hold thine hand, for my weak and sickly body is overcome.' "4

The rest of Mary's spiritual life is hidden in God's memory, but her memoir offers spiritual insights for us even today.

Mary died near the end of January 1762. She was at least eighty-four years old. Let her own words conclude her story: "I can declare . . . that wisdom's ways are ways of pleasantness, and all her paths are peace. All the paths of the Lord hath dropped much sweetness to my soul. I have often been revived and refreshed both by word and sacrament. The thousandth part of his love to me cannot be told."5 May we, by following wisdom's ways, also find God's peace and sweetness.

The following readings are from Mary's narrative, *The Spiritual Experiences of Mary Somervel.* She describes an ecstatic foretaste of heaven, a prayer-filled night in the woods, and how insomnia led her to pray with surprising results.

Part of the Sky Did Open
"When I was about ten years of age, I remember the Lord in kind love gave me a most refreshing and sweet visit and manifestation of himself. I was then a very poor and destitute orphan without father or mother, but blessed forever be the Lord who made good that word to me, Psalm 27:10, 'Though me my parents both should leave, the Lord will me uptake.'6

"At this time I was engaged in my poor weak prayers at night by the side of the house [outside] when the rest were in bed. The night was pretty dark, there being no light but what the stars afforded, which together with the temptations of Satan created some timorousness upon my spirit. This was increased by the appearance of some black thing which came rolling on the ground towards me.

"As I endeavored to pray unto the Lord to keep me, I looked up to the heavens, and there presented to my sight a very bright star, upon which I fixed mine eyes with pleasure and delight, so that in a moment every frightful phantom vanished from my mind and I was no more afraid of Satan. My soul was filled with sweet impressions of the love of God.

"There came such a sweet gale of the Spirit with light, life, love, and power on my soul, accompanied with sweet enlargement in prayer, that love and affection went up on the wings of desire to the higher house, where my heart and soul was lost, as it were, in ravishment and ecstasy, insomuch that I could very gladly have laid down my body that hour in the dust that I might attain the immediate and full enjoyment of that whereof I had such a ravishing foretaste.

"While I was praying, the glory and beauty of the higher house was emblematically held forth to me in the shining splendor of that star which shined so bright upon my face that I apprehended part of the sky did open and present such a dazzling prospect as ravished my heart and excited earnest desires to depart this life that I might be for ever with the Lord.

"Here I enjoyed such a foretaste of heaven and of the powers of the world to come, that I have oftentimes since taken pleasure in looking to the twinkling stars, and they have afforded me matter of meditation on the glory and light which is beyond and above them."[7]

Under the Shadow of God's Wings
"Upon Saturday before the close of the work [preparation for the sacrament of holy communion] I was brimful of the consolations of God, so that my crazy clay vessel could hold no more! And not being able to contain, I longed for a place where I might pour out my heart in Christ's bosom.

"When the public work was ended, I had no thought about quarters, though I was a stranger in that place, but went down to a wood a little below the church, and there retired myself in secret for a considerable time. I was endeavoring to give God thanks for what of his great goodness I had received; and being sensible I could not keep what he had given me, I thought it best to commit it to him who was able to keep it, and bestow it in the time of my greatest need.

"Being surrounded by the thick bushes of the wood, the night came on e'er I was aware, and not having bespoke quarters, I [knew] not now what to do. There was no moonlight till midnight, and I could not walk in the dark by reason of my lame foot. Besides, I was afraid either of losing or discovering to others the sweet impressions that were upon my spirits, nor was I as yet willing to break up my sweet intercourse with God in secret (which was better to me in a dark and lonely wood, than the most delicious entertainment of a sumptuous palace).

My Soul Was Ravished Within Me

"These things considered, I was willing to abide all night in the wood, but first I addressed the throne of grace to know the mind of God herein, lest hereby I should tempt providence. But it pleased the Lord to confirm my faith in his protecting goodness by the following Scriptures, Psalm 91:3, 'Surely he shall deliver thee,' verse 6, 'Thou shalt not be afraid for the terrors by night,' and Hebrews 13:5–6: 'For he hath said, "I will never leave nor forsake thee." So that we may boldly say, "The Lord is my helper and I will not fear." '

"I thought I had faith in God's word and with tears expressed myself thus, 'Lord, if my heart deceive me not, I think I have faith to believe through thy dear Son Jesus Christ thou will keep me here in this desert wood from all evil as well as in any house.' So I contented myself and thought to go about prayer.

"But Satan, who is ever busy, assaulted me with suggesting that my faith was only presumption. This put me to stand a little, but falling down upon my knees before the Lord, I requested to know whether the case was really with me as the enemy had suggested, and the Lord hearkened to my [complaint] and relieved me out of my distress by showing me that his faithfulness would be a shield and buckler unto me.

"I then resolved to risk myself upon the faithfulness of God in spite of all that the enemy could do, and that I would trust in the Lord and shelter myself under the shadow of his wings. So I went on in prayer with sweet enlargement of heart and a full gale of the spirit. O the sweet fellowship and communion I had this night with the Father and with his Son Jesus Christ!

"I was so swallowed up that I continued in prayer for the space of two hours without intermission, having access unto God and being entertained in his presence. I was filled with joy and peace in believing, and my heart was melted like wax in the midst of my bowels. Thus e'er I was aware my soul set me on the chariots of a willing people. I was then saying with the disciples, on the mount, 'Lord, it is good to be here, where I can pray and believe, believe and rejoice, rejoice and love, love and admire, admire and adore, adore and delight in God as my portion without interruption.'

"About three o'clock in the morning, I heard the noise of wild creatures but was not in the least afraid, for I had set my hope in God and was not ashamed. In him I found quiet repose, having made my bed amongst the sweet promises of his blessed word.

"Sometime before day, I turned a little drowsy. I then wrapped my head in my mantle and lay down under a bush to rest, having the heavens for my covering, the earth for my bed, the trees of the wood for my curtains, and the wings of the Almighty for my shade.

"This I may say from sweet experience: that one day or night in the presence of the Lord is better than a thousand elsewhere. O but wisdom's ways are ways of pleasantness, and all her paths are peace!"[8]

A Burden-Bearer
"I have oftentimes remarked that when I omitted to pray for Zion [the church], I would have been dead and dull in prayer. But when I remembered Zion and her afflicted mourners, I seldom if ever missed the assistance of the Spirit in a way of fervor, life and spirituality.

"I remember one night my sleep departed from me and could get no rest, but tossed to and fro in my bed. Then I enquired of the Lord of the cause, and that return came by way of fatherly reproof: 'And wouldst thou sleep when Zion's calamities are so great and the burden-bearers so few?' Then came the word also, 'The rubbish is great and the burden-bearers are few, and the strength of the burden-bearers is decayed' (Nehemiah 4:10).

"This made me very low in mine own eyes. O what am I! I am a little worth burden-bearer. O Lord, how lamentable is it that Zion hath so few of all the children she hath brought up to take her by the hand or afflict themselves with her afflictions? Many a time it has been a heavy load upon my spirits to think of the disaffection and deadness of this age and generation, and of which, alas! I myself had too great a share. Yet I can say that I never found it go better with me in prayer, than when I laid out myself to be concerned for others."[9]

My Soul Was Ravished Within Me

Reflection Questions

For centuries, Reformed people and others have practiced "creation meditation," in which they focused on something in nature—in Mary's case, the stars in the night sky—and found connections with God's wisdom, presence, and care. Relevant Scriptures are Psalm 8:3 and Romans 1:20. Why not pick up an acorn, a leaf, a shell, a blade of grass, or soil and consider how it speaks to you of God?

When you can't sleep, have you "enquired of the Lord" the cause? Has the reply ever surprised you?

God asked Mary to be a burden-bearer. Have you been asked to shoulder a burden to help relieve the "disaffection and deadness of this age"? Reflect on Galatians 6:2: "Bear one another's burdens and in this way you will fulfill the law of Christ."

Mary frequently uses the terms "ravishment" and "ecstasy" to express her mystical experience of God. (Few people experience this degree of spiritual comfort.) What type of language do you use to express your delight and enjoyment of God? If there is little joy, recall Elizabeth Cairns's "starlit path" (chapter 9), and walk in faith, trusting God's good will for you.

Notes

1. Mary Somervel, *A Clear and Remarkable Display of the Condescension, Love and Faithfulness of God, in the Spiritual Experiences of Mary Somervel* (Glasgow, 1770), pp. 41, 42. See Psalm 22:22.
2. See Malachi 4:2a.
3. Somervel, *Clear and Remarkable Display*, p. 27.
4. Ibid., p. 55.
5. Ibid., p. 58.
6. Mary quotes from memory the first or second Church of Scotland metrical psalter: either *The Psalms of David in Meeter* (Edinburgh, 1655) sig. Br; or *The Psalms of David in Metre* (Edinburgh, 1696) sig. Bv.
7. Somervel, *Clear and Remarkable Display*, pp. 9–10.
8. Ibid., pp. 14–17.
9. Ibid., p. 44.

XIV

Marion Laird, 1722–1770

Heaven on Earth

When my father was really upset with someone, he burst out with one of his favorite epithets: "fathead!" Many drivers earned the insult but never noticed; they were speeding away, tempting state troopers. It seems a cruel thing to say about someone, but perhaps it is truthful. A "fathead" is someone whose sense of self is overblown and threatens others.

A wise Scottish woman diagnosed fatheadedness as a spiritual problem. She wrestled with it most of her life. When she stopped rebelling against Christ, people wore a path to her door.

Raised in the Church of Scotland, eighteen-year-old Marion Laird was well-versed in Scripture but was troubled by the minister's sermon one Sunday in 1740. The text was 2 Corinthians 3:18: "But we all, with open face beholding as in a glass the glory of the Lord, are changed into the same image from glory to glory, even as by the Spirit of the Lord" (KJV). Marion realized she knew little of God's glory. When she returned to church the next Sunday, the preacher pressed the congregation to embrace Christ as Savior.

As she pondered her response, the Holy Spirit showed her how hostile she was to God, that her heart was "a hole full of serpents." Marion remained in turmoil the rest of the year then fell ill with a fever.

A friend came to visit, urging her to accept Christ. "I can no more believe than I can remove mountains," she snapped. The friend gently countered: "So might the man say that had the withered hand, 'I cannot stretch it out.' But he obeyed the command, and power came along with it."[1] Marion reached out in pure faith to God and was suddenly filled with peace and joy. Her spirit was healed and the fever disappeared.

Trusted Voices

Marion Laird was a family servant, mystic, and spiritual guide. Born October 23, 1722, in Bersern, western Scotland, she and her family moved to coastal Greenock, where she lived most of her life. When she was seventeen her father died and she began working as a maid. A member of the Church of Scotland, she left it in 1741, when that body was conflicted over the Patronage Act of 1712, and joined the Associate Presbytery, later known as the Associate Synod. In 1757 she became ill and was confined to her house, then, her bed, for thirteen years. She died a month shy of her forty-eighth birthday in 1770, regarded as "a very eminent saint."

After her conversion, Marion entered a long period of intense spiritual growth. She was often tempted to abandon God and to harm herself, wrestling with Satan, "the roaring lion . . . who loves well to fish in muddy waters." But she also was graced by divine sweetness, especially during four-day celebrations of the Lord's Supper: "When at the table, I got leave to behold his love shining in a cup of red wine." At another sacramental celebration, she perceived God's "heart's love to me from all eternity"[2] During these sixteen years, Marion had more struggle than calm, but she prayed, meditated, read Scripture, and endured until the rebellion in her heart weakened and her spirit was ready to behold God "with open face."

In August 1757, Marion fell ill. The doctor's healing methods did nothing to alleviate her discomfort. As it became clear that her affliction would not lift, she began to see that God was steering her to new work. People came to her for spiritual guidance. For thirteen years, this bedfast woman was sought out by great numbers of people, including ministers and complete strangers, who received, as one pastor phrased it, "very wholesome" advice. She was valued as a spiritual friend and an effective intercessor, one who sometimes prayed throughout the night for those who sought her spiritual counsel.

Marion followed Christ along the narrow way, carrying her cross of struggle and affliction, a way that leads to transformation. In mystical terms, she endured the purgative life during her struggle against doubt and temptation that lasted sixteen years. Her transition to the illuminative life was marked by growth in faith and love and a deepening desire for God's presence. In her spiritual memoir Marion records numerous occasions of God's grace during this period:

"All on a sudden, a bright display of redeeming love did with power shine in upon my soul, that I was filled with wonder at the amazing good will of God to such a rebellious, unworthy, ungrateful, and rebellious creature as I was. I came home wondering at his love, and my mouth was filled with praise and my soul with joy. I thought I could never praise God enough . . . ."[3]

Marion confides another experience, in a letter to one Mrs. Glen of Glasgow:

"In the beginning of August last, it pleased the Lord to open the treasures of joy and pleasure that are at his right hand in a very large manner, for two days together. The first day I got a very sweet view of the oneness betwixt the Father and the Son, and believers in him; 'I in you and you in me,' John 20:17. 'I ascend unto my Father, and your Father; unto my God, and your God.' O what wonderful sights I beheld of the Father in Christ!

"On the second day in the morning, I got a large view of that store of joy that is at the right hand of God: I thought I could hold nothing of it, my vents are so narrow, but a little of that new wine of consolation, in comparison of what God hath to give, would overwhelm our created faculties! O to be made like him! O to see him as he is! O what could I do but wonder at his love and sometimes invite angels and saints to praise him! Sun, moon, and stars to praise him; praise him dragons and every deep; praise him, O my soul!"[4]

In another letter, dated November 11, 1766, she recalls:

"It pleased the Lord to draw aside the veil and give me a glimpse of the glory of the whole Trinity: so exceeding great and soul-ravishing was the glory of God that shined in the face of Jesus Christ, that I was so far swallowed up in beholding that divine glory, that nature was much wasted. I had a sweet impression of that glorious sight until the next Sabbath morning . . . ."[5]

It seems likely that Marion entered into union with God by love, or what Christian mystical theology calls "the unitive way." St. Paul writes, "Anyone united to the Lord becomes one spirit with him" (*1 Cor. 6:7*). Marion had long struggled against the idolatry of self and sought a new heart from Christ. In the last few pages of her memoir she suggests that she had essentially become God-centered. Surveying her spiritual life, she comments:

"I observe, so far as I know, I neither allowed nor approved of self; so far as it prevailed, it was my burden and grief. When my sweet and . . . lovely Lord was pleased to bring me into communion and fellowship with himself, then that detestable idol of self was ready to set up its head and aspired to rob Christ of his crown and all his royal prerogatives.

"Could I then be but grieved to see my glorious Lord robbed of the glory of his grace? I loathed and abhorred myself on account of its prevailing; I cried to the Lord against it, saying, 'Let King Jesus reign, let him reign and wear the crown and possess the throne in my heart for ever. I had not peace until that detestable idol, self, was discernibly got under. . . . "[6]

The long line of souls who drew near this bedfast spiritual guide affirmed: Marion Laird was a woman highly favored by God.[7] Will you let God rid you of self-absorption so that divine love may flow through you freely and abundantly?

In the following readings, Marion grapples with self-centeredness, remembers a week of "heaven on earth," counsels a relative on how to discern the movements of the Spirit, and confesses her need of divine wisdom.

Pulling the Crown Off Christ's Head
"On sabbath morning I was in a very dead and confused frame of spirit, and O, the body of sin and death grew strong. My idols had too much room in my heart, which was like to be my death. Yet none of these sins could hinder the Lord to manifest more and more of his love to me. When I came to the ordinances [Lord's Supper], I must say to his praise, he did not disappoint me. O the sweet intercourse I got of his love!

"Whilst the Lord continued to shine upon me with the light of his countenance, my mountain then stood strong. But no sooner did he hide his face than trouble presently ensued. After this display of his goodness, I met with a sore trial for a storm and tempest of spiritual pride and that abominable thing, self.

"What name shall I give it? It is a great deceiver. It is a God-dishonoring and soul-destroying thing. Then I was afraid lest all the duties I had performed should receive no other stamp but self-seeking. I saw so much of self in speaking, so much of self in writing, that I was afraid if ever the world saw them, they would dishonor God, there was so much of self in them.

"O that abominable thing, self. O self, that woeful thing self: it will not be satisfied unless it rides side for side, so to speak, with glorious Christ. Yea, and it pulls the crown off Christ's head. O the pride of my heart, it would dethrone glorious Christ out of my heart. This was very distressing to me . . . . "[8]

Highly Favored
"This last week of April 1755 was the most remarkable for signal manifestations of his glory I ever before beheld: from Sabbath to Sabbath I had a heaven upon earth. I never experienced the like of it. I sat down under his shadow with great delight, and his fruit was sweet to my taste. One morning when I awaked out of sleep, my Beloved had withdrawn himself and was gone, whereupon I, like as the hart for the water brooks, so panted my soul after more and more communion with God.

"Upon which those words were borne in on my mind with power, John 17:24, 'I will that they also whom thou hast given me be with me where I am, that they may behold my glory.' There was such a glory shined forth brightly in these words that it filled my soul with wonder. Now I saw my will that was once wholly rebellion against God, and glorious Christ's will, sweetly complying together: for he has said, 'I will that they may behold my glory,' and my soul sayeth, 'So be it, Lord.' And these words in Luke 1:28, 'Hail thou that are highly favored, the Lord is with thee,' and Jeremiah 31:3, 'I have loved thee with an everlasting love.' "[9]

God's Love Is First
"Letter 30. To James Wilson, my Brother-in-Law.

"Loving and affectionate Brother,
"On the receipt of your [letter], I endeavored to attend to the contents of it; and therein I perceived several things.

"Ye say, 'I would know if we be lovers of our Lord Jesus.' It is true, but I am not satisfied with so general an answer. If ye be lovers of God, your love to him is a fruit of his love to you, and you have been convinced of your natural enmity against him, and see that you could never have loved him unless he had first manifested himself to you.

"Some speak as if it were natural for them to love God; poor creatures, they never saw that they were born with a dagger of enmity in their heart against God. True lovers of God have seen their [lack] of love to God and the strength and power of their enmity against him, and have gotten it broken, in some measure, in a day of his power. . . .

"Divine love acts freely. God dwells not with us upon any terms conditionally, nor valuable considerations in us. We can neither beg heaven nor buy it; it must be given us. Therefore let not the greatest civilest [person] presume nor the greatest sinner despair: God's love is first on the field. . . .

"The convictions of the Spirit are humbling . . . but the temptations of Satan tend to make the soul despair of hope in Christ or in God through him. The former shuts the door of access by the law, but Satan would shut the door of access by the gospel. . . .

"I understand you have been perplexed about the meaning of some Scriptures. Perhaps you know not well whether they came by the Spirit of God or from Satan. I will give you a note of Mr. Erskine's upon that head. He saith: 'A word that cometh from Satan bears Satan's image, which is pride and unholiness and tendeth to make a man proud and carnal. But a word from God bears God's image and maketh a man holy and humble.'[10]

" . . . Whatever your burdens are, cast your burdens upon the burden-bearer of Israel, and he will bear you and your burden both. Cast yourself over upon him, and your family upon him, and all that concerns you either for time or eternity, and he will make a good account of all that is committed to him. That the Lord may enable you by his grace so to do is the desire of your sister,
Marion Laird
Greenock, May 16, 1765"[11]

Much Need of Divine Wisdom
"I saw much need of divine wisdom to guide [me] in the middle path of judgment: I found one party in my soul that was for carnal ease . . . I found another party in my soul that said, 'That is not the way to glorify God.' "[12]

Let a Woman Ask Wisdom of God?
"One day I was in a difficulty about a duty I was engaged in. I [knew] not how to manage it, either to the glory of God or the edification of others. I went to the Lord by prayer for direction, and that Scripture came to mind: James 1:5, 'If any of you lack wisdom, let him ask it of God, who giveth to all men liberally and upbraideth not.' I was enlarged in pleading the out-making of it, and got some-

thing of a view both of the faithfulness of God and of his boundless liberality. 'And will not your heavenly Father give the Holy Spirit to them that ask it of him?' Luke 11:13.

"I was suddenly assaulted by Satan with that temptation, 'Where is it said in all the scriptures, "Let a woman ask wisdom of God"?' I [knew] not how to answer the enemy, for I did not mind a scripture that read that way. With difficulty I intended to hold fast my persuasion I had formerly attained unto.

"I believed that woman sinned in Adam and fell with him in his first transgression. I believe also that the way of their recovery out of that miserable state is by the second Adam, the Lord Jesus Christ, whom 'God hath set forth to a propitiation through faith in his blood, to declare his righteousness for the remission of sins that are past, through the forbearance of God,' Romans 3:25.

"Notwithstanding, I got not my mind fully relieved till it pleased the Lord, in his free love and adorable sovereignty, to bear in those words with a sweet refreshing power, light, and life accompanying them: 'He who spared not his own Son but delivered him up to the death for us all, how shall he not with him freely give us all things?' And, 'All are yours, and ye are Christ's, and Christ is God's,' Romans 8:32, 1 Corinthians 3:23. With these many 'all things' that God giveth with Christ, I saw that God giveth wisdom also."[13]

Reflection Questions

Not many people are mystics, like Marion, but many people have felt God's presence in a vivid way. How often do you remember this experience and allow it to affirm your faith, as Mary, Jesus' mother, pondered the words of the angels (*Luke 2:8–20*)?

Marion speaks of pride or self-will as something that rebels against God and dethrones Christ. People with low self-esteem may still be spiritually proud. Define self-will and explore what it means to seek God's will. Read John 5:30.

Marion often felt the need for divine wisdom to guide her and prayed for God's direction. When was the last time you prayed for guidance? Can you trust God with the little stuff too?

Notes

1. Marion Laird, *Memoir of the Life and Experiences of Marion Laird, An unmarried Woman in Greenock*, 2nd ed. (Glasgow, 1781), p. 16.
2. Ibid., pp. 39–40, 84.
3. Ibid, p. 49.
4. Ibid., pp. 188–89.
5. Ibid., p. 224.
6. Ibid., p. 141. Marion was not speaking of a sacrifice of self-esteem, but, rather, of a subduing of the will, so that one is "sweetly complying" with the divine will, as she says in the reading *Highly Favored*.
7. The text is revised and adapted from Diane Karay Tripp, "Singing a 'Mixed Song,' " *Horizons: the Magazine for Presbyterian Women*, July/August 2002, pp. 9–11.
8. Laird, *Memoir*, pp. 76–77.
9. Ibid., pp. 50–51.
10. Marion is referring to the work of either Ebenezer Erskine (1680–1754) or his brother, Ralph Erskine (1685–1752). Specifically, the reference might be to *The Whole Works of the Rev. Mr. Ebenezer Erskine . . . Sermons . . .* (Falkirk, 1791): "The Humble Soul the peculiar Favourite of Heaven," "The more of Christ, the more humility; and the less of Christ, the more pride," or to Ralph Erksine, "The Believer's Internal Witness," in *The Sermons and Other Practical Works* (Glasgow, 1764), vol. 2, p. 357: "Satan's witnessing doth exalt self; the Spirit's witnessing doth tend to self-humiliation . . . ." Both were Associate Synod pastors.
11. Laird, *Memoir*, pp. 214–16.
12. Ibid., p. 112.
13. Ibid., pp. 226–27.

XV

Susanna Anthony, 1726–1791

Devoted to God's Public Service in a Secret Way

Happiness seems fleeting, and misery often follows joy. An early American who endured the hardship of the Revolution believed that unhappiness is the default state of anyone alienated from God and that true happiness is a sign of divine union. Surely this is wisdom.

Susanna Anthony was born October 25, 1726, in Newport, Rhode Island, to Isaac Anthony, a goldsmith, and his wife, Mercy, a couple with seven daughters. Being of delicate constitution and prone to illness, Susanna lived with her parents some forty or fifty years until their death and helped to support herself by needlework. During the American Revolution, she left Newport for the relative safety of the countryside and lived with several families, earning her keep by teaching their children. She returned to Newport after the war and lived there the rest of her life.

As a Quaker, she was raised to wait on inner light for guidance and to love and serve the Lord. She became aware of her own sinfulness when she was about six years old and was anxious to be good and receive forgiveness. As she grew older, she became superstitious and no longer felt she was a sinner.

In her thirteenth or fourteenth year, Susanna entered a prolonged spiritual crisis precipitated in part by the death of her eldest sister. She was tempted to have nothing to do with religion until the famed Great Awakening preacher George Whitefield came to town, rekindling her inner struggle. A year later she visited Gilbert Tennent, a Presbyterian minister and revival leader, but said little, answering his questions with a simple yes or no.

Gradually her crisis began to resolve. She listened to the visiting preachers, studied religion, and became convinced that the sacraments of baptism and the Lord's Supper were instituted by Christ. The day before her sixteenth birthday, she was baptized and received into the First [Congregational] Church of Newport, sharing bread and wine at the Lord's Table.

During the service the congregation sang Isaac Watts's paraphrase of Psalm 121, music she found "very precious":

> To heaven I lift my waiting eyes,
> There all my hopes are laid:
> The Lord that built the earth and skies
> Is my perpetual aid.
>
> Their feet shall never slide to fall,
> Whom he designs to keep;
> His ears attend the softest call,
> His eyes can never sleep.[1]

In the following weeks she found peace.

Samuel Hopkins, the pastor at First Church, published extracts from Susanna's diary and letters, culled, without distorting the contents, from over one thousand pages written between 1743 and 1769.[2] He also wrote a brief account of her life and character, drawing on comments from her friends.

Susanna was not a talkative person, but she was free and open when discussing spiritual matters with close friends. They regarded her as a faithful person who kept confidences and was kind and compassionate to the poor. She prayed for others and helped those less fortunate. Her clothing was simple and unadorned, and she exercised self-control over what she ate and drank, never allowing food to render her "unfit" for prayer.

At age fifteen she joined a group of women who met one afternoon a week for prayer, Scripture reading, and spiritual conversation, and also spent four days together during the year for fasting and prayer.

The women in this group loved Susanna and informed Samuel that she was very gifted in prayer, able to pray aloud for an hour and a half with warmth and creativity. Those who prayed with her didn't weary. She was an intimate friend of another preeminent woman of the Newport congregation, Sarah Osborn, to whom she was known as "Susa."

Devoted to God's Public Service in a Secret Way

The central theme of Susanna's spirituality was her desire to conform her will to the will of God. In her words, "I rather desired to take deep root than to flourish. A humble, childlike temper did appear most desirable. I trust I heartily chose conformity to God before comfort; humility, holiness, rather than joy." "Conformity and communion with thee appears the one, the only one thing needful."[3]

Outside the church and the women's prayer meeting, Susanna was an obscure person of modest influence. Coming to terms with her frail constitution, she concluded that she could best serve Christ, the church, and others by devoting herself to prayer. On October 17, 1761, shortly before her thirty-fifth birthday, she prayed, "Set me apart for thyself."

Conscious that she could neither hold a public worship leadership role nor, as a Protestant woman, take public vows, Susanna nonetheless consecrated herself to God's service:

"Though I minister not publicly before the Lord in holy things, yet fain would I be devoted to thy service of the sanctuary in secret, solemn, and fervent supplication. Especially may I consecrate myself . . . for this service of his sanctuary that his gracious presence, assistance and influences may be granted to all his churches. God seems to be inclining my heart to this public service in a private, secret way. And blessed be God, who is inclining my heart to forsake every false way and to greater endeavors to perfect holiness . . . ."[4]

Susanna chose the one thing needful, abiding in God's presence, and her prayerfulness led other women to God. May we never underestimate the power of one soul, nestled in the embrace of the Most High, to radiate joy and trust in God to others. Though limited in the extent to which she could participate in public life, Susanna was an active, thoughtful writer. These diary passages reflect the depth of her self-dedication to God and her insight concerning the nature of happiness. She affirms God to be our only unerring Counselor.

In the Bloom of My Life
"April 1751. I hope I have most solemnly entered into covenant with God and renewedly chosen him as my everlasting portion, devoting myself entirely and unreservedly to him. And this I did in the bloom of my life, before the evil days came or the years drew nigh in which I should say, 'I have no pleasure in them.' I did it in the strength and vigor of life and health, the prime of my age. This

body was then young and active; this soul was lively in all its intellects. I did it not in a sudden fit of fear and distress; no, it was the most deliberate and rational part I ever performed.

"With all the faculties and powers of my soul, I freely, resolutely, cheerfully, and unreservedly entered into this covenant; and now, though it be far otherwise with me, yet I stand by my choice. Lord, I am fixed; thou art my chosen portion!

"And now I find myself greatly impaired, both in body and mind; my body is subjected to disease, pain, and great weakness; my mind disordered, confused, shattered, and weak, foreboding dark and dismal events, as though I should soon be deprived of my reason and rendered entirely useless, both to myself and others. Yet I am the Lord's, body, soul, and spirit, and I rely on thee, O God, to take care of thy own, in all circumstances and conditions of life. I know thou art able to keep what I have committed to thy trust against that day."[5]

The Source of Happiness
"I am more and more confirmed that there can be no true religion or real happiness any farther than the heart is really reconciled to the whole of the divine character. While there is a total alienation from the fountain and only source of perfection and happiness, there must be nothing but sin and misery. And while there is the least degree of this alienation and opposition, it must be a constant source of pollution and unhappiness, which will, in a degree, taint and interrupt all our duties and enjoyments.

"Though blessed be God, there is a foundation laid in regeneration, by slaying the opposition and enmity of our hearts, for the highest perfection and enjoyment; and as far as we are reconciled and united to God, we enter into the beginning of a state of the most perfect holiness and consummate happiness that our natures are capable of, when enlarged in the fountain of existence, to take in inconceivable communications from Deity, opening on vessels prepared for glory."[6]

Delight in God
"If I love not God supremely for himself, I am under the most fatal mistake. And my judgment must be under the power of gross darkness, unfit to be relied upon in the smallest matter, if my whole soul does not go out after God as the only suitable object of love and delight.

Devoted to God's Public Service in a Secret Way

"Here I find the most powerful attraction! Here I see all that is worthy of my regard! Hence arises my ardent desire after a perfect conformity to him, esteeming his law to be holy, just, and good, his precepts concerning all things to be right, constantly repairing to him as my only unerring counselor in every emergency of life, choosing he should rule, govern, and dispose of me and every concern of mine forever.

"Hence, I trust, my love to his people: as I love him, so I love all that is his, and all that appear in reality to love him. His people are my people, the dear chosen companions of my life."[7]

Reflection Questions

Susanna felt that overeating rendered her unfit for prayer. Do your dietary habits undermine your spirituality? How could you better integrate bodily and spiritual nourishment? Read 1 Corinthians 3:16–17.

Susanna knew that union with God is the source of happiness, and that degrees of alienation from God produce corresponding misery. Pray for closer union with God. Read John 15:1–11 prayerfully.

Susanna was gifted in prayer. What gifts has God given you? Do you cultivate these gifts, honoring the One who bestowed them? How could you be more intentional in using these gifts for others?

Notes

1. Isaac Watts, *The Psalms of David* (London, 1815), p. 196.
2. S.v. "Susanna Anthony" by Ellen Butler Donovan in *American Women Prose Writers to 1820*, vol. 200 of *Dictionary of Literary Biography*, ed. Carla Mulford (Detroit: Gale Research, 1999), pp. 28–29.
3. Susanna Anthony, *The Life and Character of Miss Susanna Anthony . . . Consisting Chiefly in Extracts from Her Writings*, compiled by Samuel Hopkins [1796] (Worcester, Mass., 1799), pp. 118, 123.
4. Ibid., p. 124.
5. Ibid., p. 56.
6. Ibid., pp. 149–50.
7. Ibid., p. 63.

XVI

Sarah Osborn, 1714–1796

Would You Advise Me to Creep into Obscurity?

"Mi casa es su casa" ("My house is your house") was the greeting my Mexican "family" uttered as I entered their home in San Luis Potosí. I was just a student, there to improve my Spanish. They embraced me as if I were a long-lost daughter. Though I was used to a two-cheek kiss from Greek relatives, "mi casa es su casa" took hospitality to deeper level: "O ancient doors!"

Perhaps Jesus' admonition to followers to make do with a pair of sandals and no change of clothes was as much about cultivating hospitality in others as trusting God.

One of the local leaders of revival in a Rhode Island town was a woman who opened her house to hundreds, if not thousands, of people. Her hospitality was a fruit of her surrender to Christ. She opened the door, and angels flooded in. Sarah Osborn, educator and spiritual guide, had an impact on colonial America unlike any other woman yet was lost to history until 1976, when a scholar came across some of her papers.[1]

She was born in London on February 22, 1714, to Benjamin and Susanna Haggar, a Congregationalist couple, and came to America when she was eight. In 1729 the family settled in Newport, Rhode Island, where Sarah lived the remainder of her life. In 1731 she married Samuel Wheaten and gave birth to a son, Samuel, whom she had baptized while her husband was at sea. He died abroad in 1733.

Widowed at age nineteen, Sarah with her infant son lived with her brother for a few months, then moved to her own quarters and began to teach.

Soon after being widowed Sarah heard a sermon by the Reverend Nathaniel Clap, pastor of First [Congregational] Church of Newport. She had a vision of her own sinfulness and turned to Clap for guidance, joining the church on February 6, 1737. In 1740 she heard the Great Awakening preachers George Whitefield and

Gilbert Tennent. After a period of distress she wrote to Tennent and received this letter in reply:

"My Dear Friend,
I like your experiences well. They seem to me to be scriptural and encouraging; and I think you may humbly take comfort from them and give God the glory of his pure grace. They who have been so humbled and distressed for sin as to be divorced from the governing love and practice of it, and have been by the Spirit of God made willing to embrace the Redeemer deliberately, unreservedly and resolutely upon his own terms, have a sure interest in the great salvation. John 1:12. To as many as received him, to them he gave power to become the sons of God, even to them that believe on his name.

"And whatever involuntary defects they are guilty of, they shall not break the everlasting covenant between God and their souls. Though they have played the harlot with many lovers, yet they may return to their first husband. Though God may hide his face for a little moment, yet with everlasting loving kindness will he return. Though they be sometimes easily beset with sin, yet he, who was the author, will be the finisher of their faith. I add no more but love and remain, your real friend, G[ilbert] T[ennent], March 22, 1741."[2]

This reassuring letter brought Sarah peace.

A number of young women from First Church turned to her for spiritual advice and asked her to provide leadership at a regular gathering. She consented, and the Religious Female Society was born. With Sarah as leader, the women met weekly for prayer, Bible reading, and spiritual conversation for fifty years. The group, which generally met at Sarah's home, was the center of First Church during the 1740s, sustained the entire church during the tenure of a later alcoholic pastor, and was crucial in renewed revival in Newport during 1766 and 1767.[3]

In 1742 twenty-eight-year-old Sarah Wheaten married Henry Osborn, a tailor and widower with several sons. Both his business and health failed within weeks of their marriage. Facing poverty, Sarah had to support the family and resumed teaching in 1744. A short time afterward, her only child, Samuel, died.

By 1766 Sarah's home had become a center of Newport religious revival. She was known as a spiritual person whom others trusted for counsel, and many people began turning up on her doorstep. At first, she didn't know what to do, but soon opened her door. The first to appear were a group of African slaves who began meeting on Sunday and Tuesday evenings for religious instruction. They numbered up to sixty or more, and a number were converted, their enthusiasm soon spreading to others. All of this should not have been a great surprise to Sarah, for since 1754 she had been interceding with God: "Of these hearts of stone raise up children unto Abraham. O let there be a shaking among these dry bones if it be thy blessed will. And, O Lord, revive religion in thine own children."[4]

Soon her home welcomed seekers every night of the week: on Mondays, young women ages nine to twenty met for prayer and instruction; Tuesdays, large numbers of boys met; Wednesdays, the Religious Female Society held regular meetings; Thursdays and/or Saturdays, she instructed children; Fridays, heads of families (generally men, sometimes women) gathered; and Saturday mornings she reserved for her soul friend, Susanna Anthony. Sarah was a spiritual leader living in a home crowded with daily gatherings at the same time she presided over a large school for children. Later, her pastor, Samuel Hopkins, observed, "Her house was indeed, and in an eminent sense, a house of prayer." She might even have been preaching in such settings.[5]

Sarah had a strong sense of abandonment or surrender to God, and viewed the nightly gatherings as the Lord's crowds. On January 27, 1767, she wrote thanksgivings to God in her diary:

"Fain would I raise a tribute of humble praise and thanksgiving for thy condescension and grace to me in the year past; for the Lord himself has vouchsafed to be my protection from errors and confusions, amidst the throng he has gathered round me. To thee be all the glory forever. In July last the number has amounted to three hundred souls. And now the Lord has increased it to five hundred and twenty five who had stately resorted here. And yet no evil has followed, though my fears have often been alarmed, with respect to Lord's day evenings, yet all is quiet and every company more seriously composed and settled in steadily pursuing after knowledge. Blessed be God . . . . O that the Lord in his infinite wisdom will carry on his own glorious work in his own gradual way which he has chosen and confound all the wisdom of the wise."[6]

As that diary entry hinted, Sarah's houseful of worshipers attracted the notice of townsfolk concerned that she welcomed teenaged boys, men, and Africans, along with women. She explained her position in a letter to Joseph Fish, a sympathetic but concerned minister, and offered to turn over leadership to any minister who felt called to the task. No one offered to relieve her of her extensive ministry. "Would you advise me to shut up my Mouth and doors and creep into obscurity?" she asked.[7] Sarah prevailed.

When the British invaded Newport during the Revolution, Sarah stayed put and continued to welcome people to her home. While many were driven into poverty, went hungry, and were harassed by soldiers, supplies found their way to her, and she was able to live in peace; soldiers took care not to disturb "that good woman."

During the last twenty years of her life, Sarah's eyesight failed and she was worn-out. A doctor's prescription of mercury earlier in life added to her discomfort. Chronic effects of mercury poisoning included nerve damage that would have progressed to severe problems with balance, walking, even paralysis. The woman whose home had welcomed hundreds of people was now confined to her bedroom. Yet, as her pastor, Samuel Hopkins, noted, this was a happy period in her life. She was serene, calm, and full of gratitude to God, seeing God's providential care everywhere. People looked after her, and though she had no savings, food, firewood, and candles arrived when needed, and friends sent her funds for rent when it was due. One time rent money arrived from the West Indies, another time from Quebec.

Sarah's long ministry with hundreds of Africans bore further fruit when Samuel Hopkins began to share in this work and took up her cause as a public antislavery advocate.[8] A number of important black Newport residents, including Obour Tanner, a close friend of the poet Phillis Wheatley, began their ministries not with a pastor, but at gatherings in Sarah's home.[9]

Sarah was left alone after her husband died in 1778, and the step-granddaughter on whom she had depended for some time moved to the countryside. One Mrs. Mason looked after her until her death.

Sarah Osborn was peaceful in old age because she surrendered her will and spirit to God:

"I am thine in Christ Jesus, and thou art mine." She had a strong sense of union with Christ and relied on the sufficiency of God's grace. "O let me bear thy image more and more, day by day, that thou mayest be glorified," she prayed.

She lived to please God, to glorify God, and to be fruitful in service. Hopkins notes that in her last years, when she could no longer attend public worship, she "enjoyed the almost uninterrupted light of God's countenance and spent most of her time and strength in devotion, in prayer and praise, in which she had unspeakable delight and a rich foretaste of heaven."[10]

Compassion, fruitfulness, and wisdom flow from hospitality to God and others. When we are bewildered by new people and strange turns in our lives, may we take heart from Sarah Osborn and receive grace to welcome the "new thing" God desires to bestow.

The following three prayers and meditation are from Sarah's *Memoirs*. In these readings we sense humility, self-knowledge, and a warm confidence in God's care.

Let Thy Grace Be Sufficient
"Ah, Lord, let thy grace be sufficient for me and I will behave as becomes a child of God, but otherwise I cannot. Lord, thou knowest I cannot, but shall act in contrariety to thee, and inconsistent with my own choice and surrenders. O, let thy grace be sufficient for me, that I may stand, that I may be steadfast and immovable, always abounding in the work of thee, Lord."[11]

An Anchor Holds Me Sure
"Without Christ I can do nothing. I am not sufficient for one good thought. All my sufficiency is of God. But God has taught me to live more by faith and less by sense than I used to do, and therefore if he hides his face, I do not immediately raze foundations as formerly and draw hard conclusions against myself.

"But having treasured up the experiences of many years, I repair to them in a dark and cloudy day and find thus and thus God has done for me and appeared for my help in times past; and this as an anchor holds me sure, and he will in his own time return and revive me. He has begun that good work in me that he will carry on till the day of Jesus. He was the Author, and he will be the Finisher of my faith. And so he makes me hang on the faithfulness of a covenant God who will not deceive nor make any ashamed of their hope that put their trust in him."[12]

Boundless Compassion
"O God, enable me to keep up high and honorable thoughts of thee, believing thou wilt be kind and gracious, believing thou wilt give grace, also believing as far as the heavens are above the earth, so far are thy thoughts above my thoughts

and thy ways above my ways. Lord, preserve me from low, mean and unworthy thoughts of thee. Suffer me not to limit thee in any wise, for soul or body, for thy compassion has no bounds."[13]

Let the Fruit be Good
"Ah, blessed Jesus, without thee I can do nothing. But am I not united to thee?
Lord, thou knowest what thou hast done for my soul.
Surely I am not among those branches which shall be taken away.
O no! thou knowest thou hast espoused me to thyself.
Thou hast engrafted me into thyself by regeneration and adoption.
O then let me not be a fruitless branch nor suffer me to bring forth sour, bitter, or tasteless fruit.
O, if the tree has been made good, let the fruit be good also."[14]

Reflection Questions
What qualities do you admire in Sarah Osborn? Where did her strength come from? Where does your inner strength come from? Reflect on Isaiah 12:2 and 40:27–31.

During her last years, Sarah experienced God's providence. Reflect on Romans 8:28: "We know that all things work together for good for those who love God, who are called according to his purpose." Consider how God has used painful or unusual circumstances in your life for good.

Sarah once prayed, "Let thy grace be sufficient for me." What does this mean? See 2 Corinthians 12:7b–10.

Would You Advise Me to Creep into Obscurity?

Notes

1. Mary Beth Norton, " 'My Resting Reaping Times': Sarah Osborn's Defense of Her 'Unfeminine' Activities, 1767" in *Signs: Journal of Women in Culture and Society* 2 (1976): 515–29. For more information on Osborn, see: Charles E. Hambrick-Stowe, "The Spiritual Pilgrimage of Sarah Osborn (1714–1796)," *Church History* 61, no. 4 (1992): 408–21; and Sheryl Kujawa, "The Teacher as Reformer: Sarah Osborn, 1714–1796," *Union Seminary Quarterly Review* 47:3–4 (1993): 89–100; also, s.v. "Sarah Osborn" by Philip Gould in *American Women Prose Writers to 1820*, vol. 200 of *Dictionary of Literary Biography*, ed. Carla Mulford (Detroit: Gale Research, 1999), pp. 268–77.

2. Sarah Osborn, *Memoirs of the Life of Mrs. Sarah Osborn*, edited by Samuel Hopkins (Worcester, Mass., 1799), p. 48.

3. Hambrick-Stowe, "Spiritual Pilgrimage of Sarah Osborn," p. 410.

4. Osborn, *Memoirs*, pp. 145–46.

5. Ibid., p. 83; Beverly Zink-Sawyer, *From Preachers to Suffragists: Women's Rights and Religious Conviction in the Lives of Three Nineteenth-Century American Clergywomen* (Louisville, Ky.: Westminster John Knox Press, 2003), p. 78.

6 Osborn, *Memoirs*, pp. 82–83.

7. Norton, "My Resting Reaping Times," p. 521. From a letter Sarah Osborn wrote to Joseph Fish around July 1766.

8. American National Biography Online, www.anb.org, "Osborn, Sarah Haggar Wheaten" by Sheryl Kujawa, p. 2.

9. Kujawa, "The Teacher as Reformer," p. 97; David Grimsted, "Anglo-American Racism and Phillis Wheatley's 'Sable Veil,' 'Length'ned Chain,' and 'Knitted Heart' " in Ronald Hoffman and Peter J. Albert, eds., *Women in the Age of the American Revolution* (Charlottesville, Va.: University Press of Virginia, 1989), p. 372.

10. Osborn, *Memoirs*, pp. 220, 303, 360.

11. Ibid., p. 285.

12. Sarah Osborn, *The Nature, Certainty and Evidence of true Christianity. In a Letter from a Gentlewoman in New England, to Another her dear Friend, in great Darkness, Doubt and Concern of a Religious Nature* (Boston, 1755), p. 10.

13. Osborn, *Memoirs*, p. 256.

14. Ibid., p. 246.

XVII

Phillis Cogswell, 1720s–1790s

I Will Come to Christ for Rest

As my mother tells it, my youngest sister, Marie, was forever running after her older sisters, yelling, "Wait for me, guys!" I can't recall if we ever slowed down. Marie had to make her own way to wherever it was we were going, whether to the neighbor's swimming pool or the frozen river. Now, as then, if there's fun to be had, we don't want to be left behind.

We don't like to see people passing us by. Phillis Cogswell, a slave in colonial New England, knew that feeling, too.

Born sometime in the 1720s, Phillis was owned by William Cogswell of Ipswich, Massachusetts, and willed to his son, Jonathan, a member of the Second [Congregational] Church of the same town. Phillis sought membership in Fourth Congregational Church, a Strict Congregational church that welcomed warm religious expression. As scholar Erik R. Seeman notes, an evangelical church was one of the few places where an African American woman could join a predominately white church during this period.[1]

When the Great Awakening of the early 1740s reached New England, Phillis saw others being saved all around her and feared being left out.

When the Seacoast Revival of 1763–64 reached Ipswich, Phillis went to worship at the meetinghouse one evening but her heart was dull and she felt disappointed. As she sat down and looked out on the evening sky, the Spirit brought Scripture to mind: "Paul may plant and Apollos water, but it is God that giveth the increase."[2]

Phillis walked home and went to bed. Just before falling asleep she soothed herself with "A Cradle Hymn" by Isaac Watts:

Hush! my dear, lie still and slumber;
Holy angels guard thy bed!
Heavenly blessings without number
Gently falling on thy head.[3]

She woke up in the middle of the night with a vision of her sins as numerous as sand on the nearby beaches and cried to Jesus for mercy and salvation. In answer, she began to feel peaceful when she read and reflected on Scripture.

One day while she was working, Jesus' words came to her: "Come unto me all ye that labour and are heavy laden and I will give you rest." "I am weary and heavy laden," she thought, "and Christ is all-sufficient to give me rest. . . . I will come to Christ for rest."

Immediately, Christ received her and she felt light, like a bird, free of her burdens. She told the Fourth Church congregation that she was a sinner who desired perfection, and she concluded her conversion story with these words: "I bless God he has given me to rejoyce with those that do rejoyce in this blessed Time of the outpouring of God's Spirit."[4]

Phillis signed the church's covenant and articles of faith on May 4, 1764, and was baptized in May or June of the same year. Her son Cesar was born that summer and baptized August 26. The next year she married Caesar Choate, a slave who was freed in 1777 and the likely father of her child. Phillis was free by 1785, and lived to be about seventy years old. She no longer looked on wistfully as others praised God and prayed with warm devotion. Christ the burden-bearer freed her to worship with heartfelt conviction.

Are we as rooted in Scripture as Phillis, so that the Spirit may use it to nourish and guide us when doubt or struggle overwhelms us? Let us seek Christ in the Word.

Here is Phillis's account of her conversion. As you read it, imagine the courage needed for a slave to confess her faith to a predominately white congregation, and consider the spiritual leap she took to rest her burdens on Christ. Now imagine taking courageous steps in your own life. Yoked with Christ, you can do all things.

I Will Come to Christ for Rest

I Felt So Light I Could Fly
"[P]hillis Cogswell . . .

"[I] was wro't upon in the former Reformation, going to [the?] meetings and see-ing others under concern, bro't me under concern fearing I should be left while others were saved; but my concern seemed to be for awhile from an apprehension that I had no convictions; but one night when I came out of the Meeting-House, I sat down and tho't how sad it was that I must leave the Meeting without receiv-ing any Benefit, but those words coming to my mind, Paul may plant and Apollos water, but it is God that giveth the increase,[5] I went home and went to bed, and the last I tho't of before I fell asleep was a couple of verses in the cradle-hymn;[6] but in the night I awaked up and all my sins seem'd to be set in order before my Eyes, and they appeared as numerous as the Sands on the Sea Shore,[7] and I cried out good Lord what must I do to be saved[8]—Jesus thou son of David have Mercy on me; and for about a week together I kept crying for Mercy, and it seem'd wonderful that I was out of hell, wonderful sparing Mercy—I was made sensible that my heart was nothing but Sin, and that I had never done any Thing but Sin against God and it would have been just with God to cast me into hell: I took to reading the Bible, and those words in Isaiah, Ho every one that thirsteth let him come to the waters, and he that hath no money let him come, &c,[9] and that, come now and let us reason together saith the Lord tho' your sins be as scar-let,[10] seemed to be comforting Texts, they came into my mind often and yet I could not get hold on them: and sometimes while I was reading the Bible, I sho'd be worried with a tho't that the wicked one would appear to me:—but one Day while I was about my work those words came to my Mind, come unto me all ye that labour and are heavy laden and I will give you rest,[11] I tho't with myself, I am weary and heavy-laden, I have a burden of guilt lying on me [,] Christ is all-suf-ficient to give rest—I may come; I will come to Christ for Rest, and my Burden was immediately taken away and I felt so light as if I could fly; Christ appeared lovely to my soul—Sin appeared odious to me, and I tho't I should never sin any more; but I find when I would do good, evil is present with me and expect it will while in this Life, tho' I desire to be made perfect:—and don't allow myself in any known Sins; I desire your prayers for me and your acceptance of me:—I bless God he has given me to rejoyce with those that do rejoyce in this blessed Time of the outpouring of God's Spirit.

"Propounded April 22, 1764"[12]

Reflection Questions

Have you ever woken in the night with painful thoughts and bad memories? Try acknowledging your sinfulness to God, and pray for forgiveness and healing.

In Matthew 11:28, Jesus extends an invitation to you: "Come to me, all you that are weary and are carrying heavy burdens, and I will give you rest." What burden do you need to share with Jesus? Do you trust him to help?

Phillis said, "When I would do good, evil is present with me." What remedies do Christians have for inner conflict?

Notes

1. Erik. R. Seeman, " 'Justice Must Take Plase': Three African Americans Speak of Religion in Eighteenth-Century New England," *William and Mary Quarterly*, Third Series, vol. 56, no. 2 (April 1999), p. 404.
2. 1 Corinthians 3:6.
3. Isaac Watts, *Divine Songs* (Gainsborough, 1786), p. 65.
4. Seeman, " 'Justice Must Take Plase,' " p. 413.
5. 1 Corinthians 3:6.
6. Written by Isaac Watts.
7. Compare Judges 7:12; Joshua 11:4.
8. Acts 16:30.
9. Isaiah 55:1.
10. Isaiah 1:18.
11. Matthew 11:28.
12. Seeman, " 'Justice Must Take Plase,' " p. 413.

XVIII

Isabella Graham, 1742–1814

Grace Will Lead Me

Isabella Graham, an educator, pioneer in American benevolent work, philanthropist, and spiritual guide, was one of God's brightest lights in early America and a coworker with Elizabeth Seton, the first American-born Roman Catholic saint.[1]

She was born in Lanarkshire, Scotland, on July 29, 1742, to John Marshall, a farmer, and Janet Hamilton. Raised on the estate of Eldersley near Paisley, she received an inheritance from her grandfather when she was ten years old and used it for a good education at a nearby school. When she was fifteen, John Witherspoon was called to be pastor of her church, Leigh Kirk, and when she was seventeen, she was received into membership of the Church of Scotland.

After completing her education she married a man she adored, Dr. John Graham. A year later, John was ordered to join the 60th, or Royal American, regiment in Canada. The family was stationed in Quebec, then Montreal. John acquired two Native American girls, Diana and Susan, to handle domestic work. Isabella became pregnant with their first child, took French lessons, and immersed herself in an expensive lifestyle.

Writing to a friend back in Paisley on August 27, 1767, John observed, Isabella's "taste is rather more refined since she came to town and turned [into] a fine lady, every day dressed out as for an assembly, introduced to colonels, majors and captains." But when Isabella began to question their household finances, she encountered resistance: "I have often begged the Doctor to save at least what he makes by his practice; but his answer is, 'Bell, we will be as frugal as we can, but we must be genteel . . . .' "[2]

The family moved to Fort Niagara, New York, where John was stationed for four years. It was the happiest period of Isabella's life. She took walks along rivers and through virgin forests near Niagara Falls. Two more daughters were born.

Trusted Voices

In 1772 the Royal American regiment was ordered to Antigua in the West Indies. In 1773, Isabella complained to her mother that they had saved little money and confessed she worried a great deal about their situation. In the fall of 1774, John was seized with a tropical fever and died. Now Isabella was alone with three daughters age five and under, pregnant, and cut off from family. She discovered that their savings amounted to only about two hundred pounds.

Friends advised her to sell the Native American girls, her husband's property, but she refused to "make merchandise of her fellow creatures." One chose to remain in Antigua; the other accompanied Isabella to Scotland and later married.

Isabella, her children, and her Native American friend boarded a ship bound for Belfast. As the ship neared its destination, a great storm arose and the ship wrecked. Toward morning it came to rest on a sandbank. They arrived at her father's cottage home a few days later.

She lived in Cartside for three years, supporting herself, her father, and family. The small British officer's pension she received was not enough to afford them more than porridge and potatoes. She churned and sold butter, made muslin dresses for sale overseas, and opened a small school in Paisley. A while later a friend suggested that she open a boarding school for young women in Edinburgh. Isabella set aside a day for fasting and prayer to seek God's guidance. As she read her Bible, she was led to John 21:15, "Feed my lambs." She opened the school in 1779 or 1780 and was a tireless and successful teacher. As her own situation improved, she founded the Penny Society, a mutual aid organization that later was renamed the Society for the Relief of the Destitute Sick.

In July 1789, with the encouragement of John Witherspoon, her former pastor and the only minister to sign the Declaration of Independence, she left Scotland, immigrated to America with her family, and opened a school in New York City. Her classroom started with just five students but numbered fifty within a month. By 1792 she had sixty scholars, plus a houseful of boarders, and taught both blacks and whites on Sunday evenings.

In 1797, Isabella, along with Elizabeth Seton and several other women, founded the Society for the Relief of Poor Widows with Small Children, one of the first such relief organizations in the United States. New York was in transition from a colonial city to an industrial metropolis. The population tripled from 1790 to 1800, and the number of helpless and destitute adults and children was exploding.[3]

Grace Will Lead Me

Isabella Graham, the society's first director, addressed the organization in April 1800, noting that the society had 141 widows and 406 children under age twelve on its books. When they were widowed, some women lost their homes and any comforts they had enjoyed, and had no food to give their children. "Every avenue to hope is shut."[4]

The society provided widows with flour, wood, flannel, and shoes and gave extra provisions to the sick. Cash allowances were granted in very unusual circumstances. Members counseled their charges and gave them moral and religious instruction, in addition to offering them employment as teachers and seamstresses or in the laundry business.

In 1798 Isabella retired from teaching but continued to direct the society and to call on widows, offering practical and spiritual counsel, as well as financial gifts. She accompanied the city missionary, Rev. John Standford, to New York's almshouse, hospital, state prison, and asylum for the mentally ill, where she visited women and children and offered spiritual support and instruction.

In 1806 she chaired the first meeting of the Orphan Asylum Society, founded by her daughter, Joanna Bethune, and served as one of its trustees and teachers. This agency clothed, fed, and taught children and placed them with families. In 1811 a group of men established the Magdalen Society and chose her to preside over its board, an office she held until her death. In 1812 she began giving catechetical instruction to students one afternoon a week. And in the spring of 1814 she founded the Society for the Promotion of Industry Among the Poor, which provided work for around five hundred women.

A few months before her death, she formed a Sunday school for young women working at nearby factories that met at 8 A.M.

A neglected aspect of Isabella's story is her friendship with Catherine Ferguson (see chapter 22). Isabella may have been the "benevolent lady" who helped to purchase her freedom; Isabella's son-in-law, Divie Bethune, provided the remaining funds. Catherine belonged to the same church as Isabella and received support and encouragement from her in her own ministry of providing students religious instruction on Sundays. Catherine also took in many orphans and found homes for others. We are poorer for having lost the story of their friendship and collaboration.

Trusted Voices

Isabella was the unofficial face of New York City philanthropic women and one of the leading figures of efforts to assist the poor.

Let us look at Isabella Graham's inner life. As a carefree child in Scotland she delighted in prayer. When she was nine years old she chose a bush in the woods under which to pray and devoted herself to God. It was a site to which she returned whenever she was troubled or wanted to mull things over. In public worship and personal and household devotion, she heard and read Scripture, learned to meditate on Scripture, sang psalms, and prayed, a solid foundation that would serve her well.

As a young woman, Isabella began writing occasional "Devotional Exercises." In an August 1796 reflection, she prayed, "Empty me of everything that is mine own and let Christ live in me, the hope of glory, and let the glory of thy workmanship in my soul redound to thee and thee alone!"[5] Throughout her life she sought to surrender herself to God in humility and trust. She never considered herself liberated from a self-centered personality, though her son-in-law, Divie Bethune, believed that self was so absent from her motives that she inspired love and respect in all those around her.

When she arrived in New York, she joined the Scotch Presbyterian Church, one of the largest congregations of the Associated Reformed Church. When Dr. John Mason died in 1792, his son, John Mitchell Mason, succeeded him as pastor. In 1810 the church moved from Cedar Street to Murray Street.

The fatal illness of Isabella's husband precipitated a spiritual reawakening. She became acutely conscious of herself as a "transgressor, rebel, idolater," and as he weakened, she prayed incessantly at his bedside. The Gilbert family of Antigua and other pious Methodists took her under their wing, comforted her, and prayed with her. On her knees the better part of five days and nights until John died, Isabella felt God's mercy surround her and rekindle hope. Concluding her reflection that Sunday evening, she turned to Psalm 98: "O sing unto the Lord a new song, for he hath done marvelous things."

As Isabella began to provide for her family and discovered her calling to teach and to help widows and their children, friends and acquaintances began to turn to her for spiritual counsel. Margaret Walker of Scotland was one friend who trusted Isabella's guidance. Another person was "P.," to whom Isabella wrote a number of letters. In the fall of 1805, after her friend had suffered a bereavement, Isabella reminded P. of Christ the friend everywhere present:

"This Friend receiveth sinners—casts out none who come to him. . . . He receives them into his heart; he takes all their burdens and cares on himself, pays all their debts, answers all demands against them, and is in every way Surety for them: they become his own; no one has anything to say to them, but himself. . . .

"In the mean time, he requires them to confide in him, to go up through this wilderness, leaning upon him, to tell him all their complaints and griefs, and to comfort themselves, and he will impress the comfort by means of his great and precious promises, scattered like so many pearls through his sacred Bible, tabled there, on purpose for us to ground our prayers upon and delight ourselves in. This is your friend's Friend, and of ten thousand beside. This was Magdalene's Friend, this the persecuting Paul's Friend, wicked Manasseh's friend, the adulterous murderous David's Friend. And he is your Friend, though your eyes are holden that you see him not. He is leading you by a way that you know not. This is one of his [characteristics], 'I will bring the blind by a way that they know not.' "[6]

On a Sabbath around 1812, when Isabella was seventy years old, she listened to a minister preach to convicts in the state prison. Sitting down to write later that day, she entered into profound reflection: "O Lord, thou knowest I stand, in my own estimation, a sinner, the chief of sinners." Painful memories of her life in Canada and Antigua before her husband's death filled her with shame. She accused herself of "smothering the heavenly spark" and "indulging to the utmost bound of lawful pleasure," while forgetting her need of God's grace. "I became cold," she continued, "negligent in the use of means, and distant in prayer," as well as "madly fond of pleasure." "Other loves usurped the place of that Beloved who had bought me with his own blood and betrothed me to himself." She felt that her heart had been crusted over and that her spiritual life had become "scarcely discernable." She remembered a premonition she'd had: "I expected affliction long before it came . . . . At last, it came . . . ."[7]

In her last years Isabella suffered from arthritis, and her memory began to deteriorate; still, she considered herself basically healthy. She lived with her daughter and son-in-law, Joanna and Divie Bethune, in a comfortable room from which she could see brooks and woods, flowers, fruit trees and shrubs. A carriage came for her on the Sabbath and during the week to take her to worship.[8] She witnessed her grandchildren become church members. Basically content, she was puzzled by periods of weeping. She continued to set aside days for fasting and prayer in order to discern her heart and prayed for God to crucify her sins.

In one of her last devotional exercises Isabella confessed that her spirit was arid and cold, but she held on to Christ in faith. It is possible that God led her into a brief night of the senses to purify her from dependence on consolations of the Spirit. On July 17, 1814, ten days before her death, she received communion at church and felt Christ's presence. The morning sermon was based on 1 Peter 1:8–9: "Although you have not seen him, you love him; and even though you do not see him now, you believe in him and rejoice with an indescribable and glorious joy, for you are receiving the outcome of your faith, the salvation of your souls."

After Isabella's death, a small manuscript of hymns and Scripture was found in her pocket. The manuscript was titled "Provision for My Last Journey through the Wilderness and Passage Over Jordan." Among the hymns was "Amazing Grace":

Through many dangers, toils, and snares
Already I have come:
T'was grace that brought me safe thus far,
And grace will lead me home.[9]

Isabella's life is a study in contrasts: poverty and wealth, loneliness and companionship, spiritual emptiness and fullness, a life of leisure followed by energetic activism. God led her from one extreme to the other, evening out her rough places that she might become a faithful shepherd, feeding Christ's lambs. May God so guide us that we too may come through heights and depths to spiritual balance and fruitfulness, faithful shepherds of those entrusted to our care.

The first of the following excerpts comes from one of Isabella's letters of spiritual counsel to a young man upon his joining the church. The other three are from her "Devotional Exercises"—meditations, prayers, and journal entries. In each passage she reveals firm trust in God's power and wisdom. She stresses the necessity of turning to God with childlike faith, expecting all good things from God, knowing that all efforts to secure ourselves blessings are futile.

Grace Will Lead Me

We are Surrounded with Mysteries
"September 1798.
"My Dear Young Friend,
"You have now ratified in a public manner that transaction which, no doubt, passed previously in private between you and your God. You have declared your belief in the gospel and have taken hold of God's covenant of promise. . . .

"You have entered the school of Christ and have much to learn, far beyond what men or books can of themselves teach, and you have much to receive on divine credit, beyond what human reason can comprehend.

"I would recommend to you to read carefully, and pause as you read, and pray as you read, for the teaching of the Spirit—the Epistle of Paul to the Ephesians. Read it first without any commentary, and read it as addressed to you, S—A—. You will there find . . . what far surpasses your comprehension. But yet read on with conscious weakness and ignorance and absolute dependence on divine teaching. When you have read it through, then take Brown's or Henry's exposition of it.[10]

"A degree of mystery, my son, runs through the whole of God's revealed word; but it is His, and to be received with reverence and believed with confidence because it is His. It is to be searched with diligence and compared; and, by God's teaching and the assistance of his sent servants, the child of God becomes mighty in the Scriptures.

"Let not mystery stagger you; we are surrounded with mysteries. We ourselves are mysteries inexplicable. Nor let the doctrine of election stagger you. How small a part of God's ways do we know or can comprehend—rejoice that he has given you the heritage of his people [and] leave the rest to him. 'Shall not the Judge of all the earth do right?'[11]

"Jesus took once a little child and set him in the midst of the people and said, 'Except ye be converted and become as little children, ye cannot enter the kingdom of heaven,' intimating, with what simplicity and docility men ought to receive the gospel, and the following text also alludes to this: 'Suffer little children to come unto me, and forbid them not, for of such is the kingdom of heaven.'[12]

"There are many promises made to the diligent searchers after truth: 'Then shall we know if we follow on to know the Lord.' 'The secret of the Lord is with them that fear him, and he will show them his covenant.'[13] Yet the highly enlightened Paul calls the gospel a mystery and godliness a mystery; for now we see through a glass darkly, but then face to face. Now I know in part, but then (in heaven) shall I know even as also I am known.[14] Therefore, while you use all diligence accompanied with prayer and the expositions of God's faithful ministers to understand every part of divine revelation, be neither surprised nor disheartened at the [lack] of comprehension, far less attempt to reduce it to human reason, as many have done to their ruin.

"The Scripture says, 'Vain man would be wise, though born like the wild ass's colt.' 'The wisdom of this world is foolishness with God.'
"I[sabella] Graham"[15]

The Gift Must First Be Received
"Christ himself, his person as well as his work, is the gift of God to sinners, to be their head, their husband, their life, as well as their prophet, priest, and king. . . . But the gift must first be received by the sinner, as a sinner, then the promise follows, or rather, goes with it, 'power to become his child.'[16]

"It is in the first act of simple faith that I think my friend has come short, not of eternal life—no, faith she has long had to be saved—but has not entered into present rest. He that hath entered into rest hath ceased from his own works, as God did from his. You have kept looking for evidences in yourself instead of crediting the invitation and the promise. It is not God's ordinary way to give such evidences. The man with the withered hand might as reasonably have said, 'Lord, let me first feel strength, and then I will believe that I shall be able to stretch it out.' . . .[17]

"Try now to rest on the promise; keep to it: 'Though he slay me, yet will I trust in him,' and take the gift of God for the foundation of your rest. . . .[18]

"You change, but God never. Satan desired to have you, that he might sift you as wheat, but Christ prayed for you. Temptation may return, but hold fast the promise. God giveth to you eternal life. Be assured, the more firmly and steadily you can believe this, the more you will grow in love to God and all holy obedience. Watch against doubts; they come from the enemy, and listened to, they give him great advantage over you, for faith is your shield."[19]

Grace Will Lead Me

Be to Me Memory

"Blessed Comforter, thou seest old age upon me, loss of memory, and a desultory mind. I cannot retain even the substance of my dear pastor's sermons. I thank thee for the food and refreshment at the time, and often for refreshing meditations on the same subjects. I commit all to thee. Keep them for me and feed me with these truths as thou seest I need. Be to me memory, judgment, presence of mind, for order and regularity and the vigor of my natural powers are gone. I rejoice in my dear Savior, who of God is made unto me wisdom, righteousness, sanctification, and complete redemption. He shall perfect that which concerneth me and finish the work he has begun. Therefore I say, all is well."[20]

Faith is All That Supports Me

"Isaiah 50:10. 'Who is among you that feareth the Lord, that obeyeth the voice of his servant, that walketh in darkness and hath no light? Let him trust in the name of the Lord and stay himself upon his God.' To trust in the name of the Lord and to stay myself upon my God is still my privilege and (though with little life and little comfort) my experience. My mind is so desultory, that my Bible and the helps derived from men's deductions and experiences seem useless. They are not often blessed as means to fix my heart. Trifles of every sort pass and repass often. While mine eyes read the words, my mind is gone in a dream on some other subject; my heart remains unimpressed, my mind, uninformed, the same in prayer, especially in secret and in the family, less so in the sanctuary.

"I seem, as to apprehension, left to my own dark, dismal, carnal self. Naked faith on the finished work of my Redeemer is all that supports me, and that as a bare preventive of fear and source of hope that I shall yet praise him who is the health of my countenance and my God. I know that his covenant stands fast. . . . I do, as this cold and stupid moment, place my confidence in it. Christ is God's covenant, God's gift to sinners; I believe it. He is the Lamb of God, which taketh away the sin of the world; I believe it: I believe on the Son for all the purposes for which God hath sent him into the world; therefore I have everlasting life. I believe the record that God gave of his Son—that God hath given to me eternal life and this life is in his Son, not in me, but in union with him. 'He that hath the Son hath life. He that hath not the Son hath not life.' 1 John 5:12.

"I thank thee, my God, that thou hast not left me to cast away my confidence in Christ. I have life in him, and no life but as I have it from him."[21]

Reflection Questions

Isabella reminded an acquaintance of Christ, "the friend everywhere present." Reflect on John 15:14: "You are my friends if you do what I command you." Christ is your friend. Do you confide in him?

Isabella wrote, "We ourselves are mysteries inexplicable. . . . How small a part of God's ways do we know or can comprehend?" Does this comfort or upset you? Why? What Scripture passages does this bring to mind? Read Isaiah 55:6–9.

When Isabella was coping with memory problems, she nonetheless prayed, "All is well." Why could she make this affirmation? Does this change your perspective of the problems that face the elderly?

Notes

1. *Notable American Women, 1607–1950*, vol. 2, ed. Edward T. James (Cambridge, Mass.: Belknap Press of Harvard University Press, 1971), pp. 71–72; Page Putnam Miller, *A Claim to New Roles*, ATLA Monograph Series, no. 22, ed. Kenneth E. Rowe (Metuchen, N.J.: American Theological Library Association and Scarecrow Press, 1985), pp. 35, 84–93, 96–97; s.v. "Graham, Isabella" by Thaddeus Russell in *American National Biography*, vol. 9 (New York: Oxford University Press, 1999), pp. 379–80.
2. Isabella Graham, *The Unpublished Letters and Correspondence of Mrs. Isabella Graham*, edited by [Joanna] Bethune (New York, 1838), pp. 17, 32.
3. Dorothy G. Becker, "Isabella Graham and Joanna Bethune: Trailblazers of Organized Women's Benevolence," *Social Service Review* 61 (June 1987): 323.
4. Isabella Graham, *The Power of Faith: Exemplified in the Life and Writings of the Late Mrs. Isabella Graham, of New-York*, compiled by Divie Bethune and Joanna Bethune (New York, printed; London, reprinted, 1816), p. 457.
5. Ibid., p. 111.
6. Isaiah 42:16; ibid., pp. 327–28.
7. Ibid., pp. 194–95, 197.
8. Weekday public worship was observed morning and evening in a few large American cities, following a long-established tradition that derived from European Reformed churches, including the Church of Scotland.
9. Graham, *Power of Faith*, p. 274. "Amazing Grace" was written by John Newton (1725–1807).
10. Prayerful Scripture reading, or *lectio divina*, was long practiced by people of the Reformed tradition. Books she may have had in mind: John Brown, *The Self-Interpreting Bible Containing the Sacred Text of the Old and New Testaments*, 2 vols. (Edinburgh, 1778); Matthew Henry, *An Exposition of All the Books of the Old and New Testament*, 6 vols., 3rd ed. (London, 1721–1725).
11. Genesis 18:25.
12. Matthew 18:3; 19:14.
13. Hosea 6:3; Psalm 25:14.
14. She alludes to Ephesians 6:19; 1 Timothy 3:16; and 1 Corinthians 13:12.
15. See Job 11:12 (KJV); 1 Corinthians 3:19. The reading is from Graham, *Unpublished Letters*, pp. 236, 238–41.
16. See John 1:12.
17. See Matthew 12:9–13.
18. Job 13:15.
19. Graham, *Power of Faith*, pp. 333–35. From a letter to "P.," August 24, 1810.
20. Ibid., p. 214. From a devotional exercise dated April [1812].
21. Ibid., pp. 223–24. From a devotional exercise dated 1814.

XIX

Fanny Woodbury, 1791–1814

Make God Your Friend

Some people feel good to be with, while others make us feel anxious and confused. Psychologists urge us to avoid these "toxic" people and to spend more time with those who are supportive. Christians seek to grow out of sin—toxicity—into the image of Christ, the one who radiates peacefulness and opens his arms wide to all. Fanny Woodbury was a young woman to whom others were drawn. They sensed her communion with God and felt nurtured in her presence. Her writings convey this same peacefulness and promise.

Fanny was a devout Congregationalist born September 10, 1791, to Isaac and Anna Woodbury of Hamilton, Massachusetts. When she was three Fanny contracted a fever that left her with recurring deafness. Despite the affliction, she attended Bradford Academy and experienced conversion while a student there.

On September 27, 1807, at age sixteen, she joined the Second [Congregational] Church of Beverly, Massachusetts, and was the youngest member of that church until her death from an illness at age twenty-three.

She did a lot of housework for her family and devoted the rest of her time to God through prayer, counseling and praying with those in need, visiting the poor and sick in their homes, and sewing dresses for women as an act of charity.

A shy and reserved person, she found comfort in solitude and loved to pray every morning, noon, and night on her knees. She also meditated, read Scripture, sang hymns and psalms, and read religious books, including *The Rise and Progress of Religion in the Soul* (1st ed. 1745) by Philip Doddridge and Daniel Dana's edition of *Memoirs of Eminently Pious Women* (1803). She kept a journal and wrote letters of evangelical counsel and guidance to friends and relatives.

Trusted Voices

She was gifted beyond her years in understanding and had a sense of being called to spiritual direction. In November 1813, she wrote to Nancy I. of Beverly:

"O pray for me, that I may have an insight into the complicated windings and shiftings of the human heart, and an acquaintance with spiritual experiences, that I may be qualified to speak a word in season to the various cases I meet with, but especially that after preaching to others, I myself may not be a castaway."[1]

Others sensed that she could be trusted and relied on her for guidance. It is certain that had she lived longer, the numbers of those she counseled would have grown.

Spirituality so permeated her heart that when parting from friends, she would often say, "Do live near to God" or "Pray much and fervent." Letters to others opened with similar intent: "How does your soul do this morning, my dear Sally?" she asked her cousin in 1813. To another she wrote, "Does your soul prosper?" Fanny stressed the importance of intimate friendship with God: "O make God your friend and heaven your home." She also emphasized reliance on Christ: "We must place our whole dependence on Jesus. He is all-sufficient, and if we repair to him for grace and strength to do his will, he will not deny us."[2]

"Love and humility are the quintessence of religion," she once wrote to a friend. These same qualities were abundant in Fanny Woodbury, a gifted young woman devoted to comforting and guiding others. May the Holy Spirit nurture the gifts of love and humility in us that others may find us to be trustworthy spiritual friends.

The following are excerpts of two letters of spiritual guidance Fanny wrote to a friend in 1813. She encourages her friend to be less self-absorbed and to focus simply on Christ and assures us that by anchoring ourselves in God's love we will be more tranquil in the face of unsettling changes.

Live More Simply in Christ
"Letter to Miss M. S. of Chelmsford [Massachusetts], Beverly, Aug. 6, 1813.

"My dear and much loved Miss S.
"My earliest acknowledgements and ardent thanks are due for your very affectionate and obliging letter and the freedom with which you have opened your heart to one who will cheerfully reciprocate your confidence, but laments her inability to establish, strengthen, stimulate and direct you as she ardently wishes.

Make God Your Friend

"You do not appear to enjoy that evidence of your union to Christ and those elevated and rapturous feelings with which you have formerly been favored in some previous moments, and for which you now aspire. Yet I trust you retain a comfortable hope that you have passed 'from death unto life.' I think we are too easily elated with raised affections, and then, when they subside, though we may be equally in the exercise of grace, unreasonably depressed; whereas we ought to regard more the habitual disposition of our minds. Frames and feelings are variable and inconstant, but God never changes.

"I do believe it would be better with us generally if we kept Christ more in view and lived more simply and entirely on him and less engrossed with our little selves. Let us, my dear friend, strive for a confidential trust in him and solid evidence that we are his disciples, and then let not every discouraging appearance, every temptation of the adversary, disconcert and unsettle our minds and throw us into yielding [to] timidity and gloomy despondency. The best way to get rid of our doubts and fears is to engage resolutely in what we know to be duty, however crossing to our natural propensities, and to renounce all known sin and avoid every appearance of evil, though it should subject us to many mortifications and trials . . . ."[3]

Like Mary at the Feet of Her Redeemer
"Letter to Miss M. S. of Chelmsford, Beverly, Oct. 29, 1813.

"As I again direct my thoughts to Chelmsford, my heart solicitously inquires into the concerns of my beloved fellow pilgrim there and tenders its most ardent and affectionate wishes for her progress in the Christian race. . . .

"May this find you, my dear sister, not like Martha of old, cumbered with the affairs of this vanishing world, but, like gentle Mary, at the feet of your beloved Redeemer, imbibing his spirit and drinking his instructions, and solacing yourself under the banner of his love. . . .

"You will recollect that the arm of the Lord is your strength, and that you cannot take one step nor even stand the ground you have gained, but by the special assistance of almighty grace. O how often do we stumble and fall through self-dependence, self-love, and self-sufficiency, and thereby grieve the blessed Jesus and bring leanness into our souls; and surely, if superior power did not raise us, we should there remain, wallowing in the slough of despond, and sinking deeper and deeper in the mire, or reaching the city of destruction, take our station there, with wrath impending over our guilty heads.

"But blessed be God, that he has engaged to perfect the work which he begins, and that by a mighty power and stretched-out arm, he will bring all his soldiers from the field of battle with songs of victory on their lips and triumphant joy in their hearts. A true Christian may fall frequently, may fall grievously, but shall never fall finally. O no. The grace, the love, the power, the faithfulness of Jesus are engaged to bring every newborn soul home to glory in defiance of all the hosts of hell."[4]

Reflection Questions

Fanny asked a good friend to pray for her work of spiritual guidance. Do you have a friend for whom you can pray, one who will support you in prayer? What benefit do you see in having a spiritual friend?

Fanny counseled a friend that "feelings are variable and inconstant, but God never changes." Compare this statement with Jesus' imagery in Matthew 7:24–27: the house built on sand and the house built on rock. Which house would you rather live in? How can you make Christ the foundation of your life?

Why do you suppose Fanny said that the best way to get rid of doubts and fears is to do one's work with energy and to avoid sin and evil? What other means do we have to overcome fear and doubt?

Notes
1. Fanny Woodbury, *Writings of Miss Fanny Woodbury*, edited by Joseph Emerson (Boston, 1815), p. 194.
2. Ibid., pp. 146, 112, 263, 47.
3. Ibid., pp. 174–75.
4. Ibid., pp. 187–88.

XX

Hannah Sinclair, 1780–1818

Growing in Grace and Knowledge

When I was about thirteen, I approached our pastor between services and said, "Scripture says 'God is love' and 'Love is not jealous,' and then in the commandment, 'I am a jealous God.' I don't understand." In my mind these contradictions implied that God was not love or that some Scripture was not true. He reassured me.

Those of us who get confused and muddled need others with clear minds to teach us. Hannah Sinclair was such a teacher, gifted with insight.

She was born February 1, 1780, in Ulbster, Caithness County, Scotland, to Sir John Sinclair, a baronet and member of the British Parliament, and Sarah Maitland, who died when her daughter was five years old. She was raised by her grandmother, Lady Janet Sinclair, in Thurso Castle, "a stormy mansion" perched on the coast overlooking Pentland Firth.

Lady Janet took Hannah and her sister Janet to church and helped them learn the Shorter Catechism. Their English nurse gave the two frequent affectionate Bible lessons. Hannah had an insatiable thirst for knowledge and by age ten had read many books in her father's extensive library. She preferred reading to playing outdoors and liked to quiz visiting ministers and other learned people with hard questions.

When Hannah was eleven, Lady Janet moved her two granddaughters to Edinburgh, where they attended the Canongate kirk. One of the ministers there, Dr. Walter Buchanan, impressed the girls with his warmth and kindness. Until they met him, they had thought religion was all about restraint and strictness. The sisters were captivated by the pastor's gracious sermons and spirituality. Two years later, Hannah's grandmother took her and Janet to Stoke Newington, near London, and enrolled them in the boarding school that their mother, Sarah, had attended before them. Hannah was an excellent student and especially enjoyed her astronomy course but found few friends who shared her intellectual passion.

When Hannah was sixteen, and Janet, fifteen, they returned to Edinburgh and were introduced into high society by their stepmother, Lady Sinclair; the sisters began to attend parties and to meet young men. At the same time, they resumed attending divine service at Canongate. Although Hannah had long observed the traditional ritual of personal prayer common in the Church of Scotland—prayer, meditation, Scripture reading, and psalm singing—she became more devout and regular in her prayer as she began to contemplate spiritual concerns. Her foremost question was "What must I do to be saved?"

One day Hannah found a new book on her father's desk, *A Practical View of the Prevailing Religious System of Professed Christians* (1797) by William Wilberforce, a friend of their father and leader of the evangelical wing of the Church of England. She carried it off to her room and read it, delighted to recognize the same evangelical doctrine preached by their beloved pastor, here set forward with simple eloquence.

This book taught her to receive Christ and to rely on him. She had doubts and anxiety about doctrines such as free will and predestination and turned to her sister Janet for counsel. Janet urged her to seek her Savior in prayer and guided her toward a spiritual relationship with God. Hannah began to regulate her life by the scriptural idea of doing everything to the glory of God and made biblical spirituality her foremost concern.

Hannah was indifferent to society life and its finery, preferring to live more simply. When she was twenty years old, her sister married Sir James Colquhoun and became Lady Colquhoun. Hannah set herself the task of teaching her half-brothers and half-sisters, her father's second family. In 1806, when she was twenty-five, she had a hard time shaking off a cold and showed the first symptoms of consumption. By this time her theological questions were resolved; she trusted her Savior.

In 1814, John Sinclair moved the family to Ham Common in Surrey, England. Hannah regularly visited the sick and gave religious instruction to the poor. It was also here that she wrote a long letter to her half-sister, Catherine, then seventeen, explaining the heart of evangelical religion. This small book, begun October 19, 1817, and finished in a few weeks, was published some months later and enjoyed wide circulation.

In January 1818 her consumption returned. Hannah died on May 23, 1818, at age thirty-eight.

Growing in Grace and Knowledge

In an introduction to Hannah's book, *A Letter on the Principles of the Christian Faith*, John Sinclair, her father, paid tribute to her: "Nothing gave my dear daughter so much delight as doing good. . . . No one ever saw her temper ruffled or ever heard her say anything harsh or unfeeling respecting the conduct or the motives of others."[1]

In a diary she began during her last year of life, Hannah prayed, "Thou knowest that my most earnest wish is to grow in grace and in the knowledge of my God and Savior, Jesus Christ."[2] Her prayer was certainly answered. May God answer the deepest yearnings of our hearts through prayer and bless our relationships with others and the fruits of our work. Like Hannah may we find ourselves growing detached from what is superficial and lured by love toward the simple glory of God.

The following readings are from Hannah Sinclair's long letter to her half-sister, Catherine, on the subjects of sin, faith, and prayer. She invites us to root our lives in the One in whom all things become new and shows how the desire for centeredness is a gift of God.

All Things Must Become New
"The first of these [evangelical] doctrines and the foundation of all the rest is that of the deep depravity and corruption of human nature. This doctrine in the main is not, I believe, denied by any, but the evangelical preachers explain it in a different manner from what others do. By others it is considered a slight taint; by them it is represented as a deep pollution, a total alienation of the heart from God which is most culpable and wholly inexcusable in his sight.

"So far is man, in a state of nature, from loving God above all things that there is scarcely anything which he does not prefer to God. To the majority of the world, what duty is so irksome as that of prayer? What day so wearisome as the Sabbath? What time so long as that which is spent in church? What books so uninteresting as those which treat of religion?

"Besides this dislike and repugnance to the exercise of devotion, or, in other words, to all manner of intercourse with God, there is, in fallen man, a spirit of disobedience and rebellion against his Maker. It is true that many of the persons here described do fulfill various moral duties and so far obey his commands, but they do not obey them because they are his commands.

"Generally speaking, some motive of interest, pleasure or vanity or self-gratification of one kind or another secretly influences them, or, if they do pay any regard to God at all, it is the fear of his wrath which prompts them. They do not obey from a sincere filial desire of pleasing him but from dread of a power which they know cannot be resisted. Such is man by nature without any exception.

"This charge may be brought with as much justice against the decent and moral as against the vicious and profane. Nay, even the most eminent Christians, though this is no longer their character, will most readily acknowledge that it was once so. They can all of them remember a time when they were exactly in the condition here described.

"Now as God has repeatedly declared in Scripture that he will on no account admit into his presence those who are thus alienated from him, it follows of course, that if we live and die in this state we must perish forever, or to use our Savior's words, 'Except a man be born again, he cannot enter into the kingdom of God' [*John 3:3*]. The change which our Savior alludes to in these words is described in the Bible under a great variety of figures and phrases, such as 'being renewed' [*2 Cor. 4:16*] and 'sanctified' [*1 Cor. 1:2*], being adopted into the family of God [*Rom. 8:15, Eph. 1:5*], being no longer under the law but under grace, having passed from death to life [*John 5:24*], etc. and St. Paul expressly says, 'If any man be in Christ, he is a new creature; old things have passed away; behold, all things have become new' [*2 Cor. 5:17*], by which is plainly signified not only that the change must be great, but that it must be universal, 'That all things must become new.' "3

The Gift God Alone Can Bestow

"Are we then sensible that we are sinners? Let us think of the blood of Jesus and believe 'that it cleanseth from all sin' [*1 John 1:7*]. Do we, on the other hand, lament the many defects which attend even our best performances? Are we afraid that such an imperfect obedience as ours is can never be acceptable to God?

"Let us think of him who has perfectly fulfilled all righteousness and believe that his righteousness shall be imputed to us if we are only sincerely willing that it should be so. I mean if we sincerely, and from the heart, renounce all dependence upon ourselves, upon anything we have ever done or can do in [the] future, and rely solely and entirely on the Lord Jesus for pardon, salvation, and every spiritual blessing. This, believe me, is no easy matter. This is the rock upon which the great majority of the children of Adam do split and suffer shipwreck.

"It is, indeed, what none are brought to but by the effectual teaching of the Holy Ghost. For though it be easy in words to renounce all dependence on ourselves, yet to feel in our hearts how lost and undone, how guilty and depraved we are, and how incapable of ourselves of doing anything that is truly good, even of thinking a good thought, and at the same time to feel that implicit confidence and firm reliance on the Savior which the Bible requires, is one of the hardest tasks which ever was proposed to fallen man. It is so contrary to his pride and to his natural notions, and, indeed, it is so very hard a task, that we might well despair of ever being able to fulfill it, were it not for the promise of divine assistance.

"Faith, we are told, is the gift of God. This cannot well be said of a mere historical faith, but in reference to the faith I have just been describing, it is perfectly true that God alone can bestow it. The propensity to self-dependence in fallen man is so very strong that nothing less than Almighty power can completely destroy it.

"To God, then, let us apply for this faith with fervent and repeated entreaties. Like the importunate widow, let us give him, so to speak, no rest till he bestow upon us this inestimable blessing. If we do obtain it, from that moment we are safe—as safe as if we were actually in heaven. 'He that believeth in me,' says the Savior, 'hath everlasting life' [*John 3:36*].

"Observe the expression: not shall have it, but hath it already—is as secure of it as those who now enjoy it. From the moment we thus believe, Christ's righteousness is imputed to us . . . .[4]

With God All Things Are Possible
"You wish to know how this precious faith is to be obtained? How is it possible for us frail mortals, surrounded as we are with the objects of time and sense, and with a great variety of temptations, thus to live above the world—thus to dwell among heavenly objects?

"I answer in the words of our Savior, 'With men this is impossible, but with God all things are possible' [*Matt. 19:26*]. Draw nigh unto God and he 'will draw nigh unto you' [*James 4:8*]. There is no spiritual blessing whatever but may be obtained from the Almighty 'by earnest, persevering prayer.' But when you pray, beware of formality.

"Many think that when they have uttered before God a set form of well-chosen words that they have done all that can be required of them. But I would not call this praying. When you pray, you should use the same earnestness and importunity which you would employ in requesting from an earthly friend some favor which you had very much at heart. And be solicitous also for an answer to your prayers. Many pray without even thinking of an answer, and how can they expect to obtain one? Surely you would not bestow a favor upon anyone who, the moment after having asked it, turned away without waiting for a reply. If you then would really desire to be renewed and sanctified, look up daily, I might almost say hourly, to him who alone can effect this change, and examine carefully and frequently also into the state of your own mind, in order that you may ascertain whether your prayers have been heard and answered.

"If you can perceive any symptoms of this blessed change in yourself, be thankful to God and pray earnestly that you may be renewed yet more and more, and pray to him in faith, believing that what you ask of him in the name of Christ, you shall in due time receive, and this will give vigor and alacrity to your prayers.

"I have sometimes thought that real Christians may be said to possess an additional sense. They see what is invisible to others. Like Stephen they behold with their mental eyes 'the heavens opened and Christ sitting at the right hand of God' [*Acts 7:56*]. But we can no more confer on ourselves this additional sense than we can add to the number of our bodily senses. In fact, every conversion is so entirely brought about by the agency of the Spirit of God that it may be called a miracle and only differs from the miraculous cures recorded in the Gospels in this respect, that the latter were outward and visible miracles, whereas the former is an inward and invisible one.

"But here I would remind you of what happened to the blind man who was sent to wash in the pool of Siloam. Though the miracle was performed by the power of our Saviour alone, it was his pleasure that the blind man should use the means which he prescribed to him. Thus it is with us. Though God alone can convert us, we must not neglect the means of grace."[5]

Reflection Questions

Hannah believed that renouncing self-dependence in favor of reliance on the Savior is one of the hardest things a person can ever do. How does she suggest that a person obtain such faith? What can you do daily to remind yourself to depend on God?

Why does Hannah declare that every conversion is a miracle?

Hannah observed a regular ritual of personal prayer. Can you think of several reasons why this is better than praying only when you feel like it? How can you better integrate prayer into your own life?

Notes

1. Hannah Sinclair, *A Letter on the Principles of the Christian Faith*, first American edition (Richmond, 1819), pp. 4–6.
2. Thomas Gibbons, *Memoirs of Eminently Pious Women*, revised by Samuel Burder (Philadelphia, 1834), p. 695.
3. Sinclair, *Letter*, pp. 9–12.
4. Ibid., pp. 17–20.
5. Ibid., pp. 41–44.

XXI

Catharine Dimmick, 1793–1844

A Clear-Sighted Guide

My friend Carole was feeling poorly and didn't know why. The doctor found nothing unusual. After exploring several possibilities, I summoned my courage and said to her, "Your house smells strongly of mildew." "Oh yeah?" she said. She discovered a water problem in her house, and any item on which my bloodhound nose detected mildew was carried out of the house. Old clothes, a sofa, and a spare bed awaited transport to the dump. "Thank you!" she beamed at me after one sniffing session. "I couldn't smell anything!"

A few months later we were hanging out at a local restaurant. We spotted two friends and went over to say hello. They asked Carole how she was. "Better," she said, smiling. "Diane told me my house smelled." "You what!" they burst out, laughing hard, eyes dancing. "I couldn't smell the mildew; Diane could," Carole insisted, answering on my behalf. The couple left, marveling at my audacity.

Ignoring the smell would have been polite, but Carole needed honesty to help her make healthy changes. In a similar way, sometimes people need honest observations to make spiritual progress. Catharine Dimmick was a spiritual guide willing to voice hard but necessary words.

She was born January 27, 1793, in Norwich, Connecticut, to Elihu Marvin and Elizabeth Rogers. On her father's side she was related to the Mather family of Dorchester, and on her mother's, descended from the English Protestant martyr John Rogers (d. 1555). Her physician father served as a general in the Continental Army during the Revolutionary War and died when Catharine was five years old. She was baptized soon afterward in First [Congregational] Church, Norwich, an event she remembered for the rest of her life. Her grandfather, Dr. Theophilus Rogers, helped to care for the family for about three years until his death in 1801.

Young Catharine was educated at home, essentially self-taught. When her mother died in 1808, she was sent to her uncle Benjamin Snow of Norwich. Orphaned and separated from her siblings, she was thrown on her own resources.

A year after her mother's death, sixteen-year-old Catharine opened a school for young women at which she taught for six years. One of her pupils, Sarah Huntington (Smith) (1802–1836), became a missionary teacher among Mohegan Native Americans and later served at the American Mission in Beirut.[1]

Catharine's conversion was a gradual process that culminated in August 1812, and every year afterward she celebrated its anniversary. The Holy Spirit helped her to see that happiness and hope are gifts of divine grace.

Joyfully embracing Christ as Savior, Catharine was received into the Congregational church in January 1813, shortly before her twentieth birthday. "No service is like thy service,"[2] she affirmed and devoted her energies to various ministries while grounding herself in prayer, meditation, and Scripture reading. She viewed teaching as a ministry for Christ and after her conversion, thought of her students as "young immortals." She made the school more religious by opening and closing the day with prayer and conducting weekly Bible lessons.

In early 1815 she moved into the home of Richard Adams to serve as a companion for his wife and to help care for and educate their children. After several months she resigned from the school in order to give the Adamses greater attention.

In August 1815 Catharine began to teach Sabbath school and continued this for the rest of her life. With another teacher she taught a class of African American women to read the Bible. That same year she began visiting female residents of a nearby almshouse. She regularly visited the poor, aged, and sick and those in turmoil and pain, counseling them, reading Scripture with them, and praying "greatly to their comfort." Catharine's biographer contrasted her with other young women who sighed with boredom because they had nothing to live for beyond themselves.

A close friend, the missionary Harriet Lathrop Winslow, wrote of Catharine in 1819 that the people of the almshouse would unanimously affirm: "she is an angel," and "there are few more ardently devoted to the cause of Christ, and more capable, with the blessing of God, of doing much good in the world."[3] Catharine visited the women for three years, until the almshouse moved to a distant location.

A Clear-Sighted Guide

On May 4, 1820, twenty-seven-year-old Catharine married the Reverend Luther F. Dimmick, a Congregational minister, and moved to Newburyport, Massachusetts. In addition to looking after her family, Catharine extended hospitality to visitors who sought her husband's counsel, continued teaching Sabbath school, participated in a female prayer meeting, served on the Board of Managers of the Female Orphan Asylum of Newburyport, and resumed her ministry to those who were afflicted and sick. In addition, she began offering spiritual guidance to groups of males and females alongside her husband. Her insights were of great value, Luther commented: "She had the faculty of discriminating in regard to different cases, and urging the needful truth with peculiar fidelity and tenderness . . . ." He continued, "She had more than ordinary skill in directing inquirers on the subject of religion."[4]

It was not long before people turned to Catharine herself for spiritual direction. She spent much time guiding others and also wrote letters of spiritual guidance to family members and others. She took no step without seeking divine direction, and followed the promptings of the Holy Spirit.

One person she conversed with wrote, "No other one was ever so great a help to me in leading me to the straight gate . . . . She had the power of choosing out acceptable words." Her husband, Luther, further observed, "In cases of difficulty, doubt, timidity, embarrassment, she was patient and acted with good judgment and fidelity. Time, which, under some circumstances, a pastor can with difficulty spare, she could more conveniently bestow."[5]

"Never apologize for coming to see me," Catharine once wrote, "when the important interest of the soul is the object of the visit. You did not detain me from a single duty yesterday." She reassured another person, "Do not be concerned at the thought that you trouble me with the overflowings of your heart."[6]

Catharine was a clear-sighted guide who spoke as the Spirit directed her. "Selfishness is our easily besetting sin, and the source of all sin, and should be most sedulously guarded against," she wrote to one friend.[7] "J" received a letter with this counsel: "Be very careful not to grieve the Spirit, who, in the expressive language of another, is 'infinitely delicate,' withdrawing speedily from the soul when his influences are not appreciated or desired. Often use that petition of our Saviour's prayer, 'Lead me not into temptation'—and be sure not to place yourself where you have good reason to believe you can do no good, and may receive much harm."[8]

In the summer of 1831 Catharine became very ill. More bouts of illness followed in the ensuing years. She died on December 8, 1844, at age fifty-one. The women of North Church, Newburyport, erected a monument in her memory. It was engraved with Catharine's plea: "I earnestly implore grace to maintain constant activity in the service of Christ."[9]

Catharine Dimmick was one of God's shining lights. May we imitate her example, letting our light shine, boldly using the gifts God has given us, that others may be strengthened in their journey with Christ, and may we likewise reach out to others who are lost, alone, and looking for the way.

In the following readings, Catharine shares her wisdom in the form of diary entries and excerpts from letters of spiritual guidance. She invites us to consider the habits of our hearts and the role of trust and discernment in daily life.

Rebellion
"January 26 [1815]. The rebellion of our hearts consists more in their habitual temper of variance with God than we are generally aware. We are too prone to imagine ourselves innocent because the sin is not clothed in overt action."[10]

My Soul, Wait on the Lord
"September 10 [1817]. I have been making known my requests unto God in prayer, and asking, among other things, a disposition to trust in him for all that I need. Now I arise to wait. And what is 'waiting on the Lord'?

"It is, if I understand it, the suppression of a too eager desire for the blessing sought; a conviction of our impotence, ignorance and unworthiness; a willingness, if God please, to have the solicited favor delayed—bestowed in any time and way which to him may seem best; a spirit submissive—quietly resigned—even if the favor should be denied. Sweet temper, and all important! Without something of it, the greatest earthly blessings lose their relish, and fill us with satiety. But this is itself compensation for good delayed. 'My soul, wait thou only upon God, from whom thy help cometh.' "[11]

Taking Care of Our Hearts Daily
"July 12, 1828. How easy it is to wander from God and to lose the vision of spiritual objects. How easy to nourish indolence and all the evil propensities of an unbelieving heart. How easy to grow cold and negligent in duty. It is only to let

ourselves alone, and remain in a careless indecision, and it is done. If then we would have true elevation of Christian character, if we would have clear evidence of our adoption into the spiritual family, if we would have that hope which is as an anchor to the soul in life and in death, we must take care of our hearts daily; we must be watchful in little things, as well as in great ones. Little things make up the larger part of our lives and affect proportionately the formation of our character."[12]

Behold Me

"Dec. 26 [1842]. What a variety of instrumentalities does God use to draw our thoughts upward and prepare us for another scene of things, in all his works as well as in all his word, saying, 'Behold me! Behold me!' It is important that we listen to this voice and that we be often thinking of heaven and contemplating its probable employments, that we may be fitted to attain its blessedness."[13]

Reflection Questions

Catharine wrote that our hearts are often in a rut of being at odds with God. Compare this with Jesus' words: "Whoever is not with me is against me, and whoever does not gather with me scatters" (*Matt. 12:30*). Are you turned toward God or away from God? Pray for the grace to be content in God's presence.

What does "waiting on God" mean for you personally? Does God's timetable frustrate you? Reflect on this Scripture: "The Lord is not slow about his promise, as some think of slowness, but is patient with you . . . ." (*2 Peter 3:9*).

How do you take care of your heart daily? With what little things do you need to exercise greater care?

Trusted Voices

Notes

1. Susan Huntington Smith, *Memoir of Mrs. Sarah L. Huntington Smith, Late of the American Mission in Syria*, third edition, edited by Edward W. Hooker (New York: American Tract Society, 1845).
2. Catharine M. Dimmick, *Memoir of Mrs. Catharine M. Dimmick*, edited by L. F. Dimmick (Boston: T. R. Marvin, 1846), p. 26.
3. Ibid., p. 32.
4. Ibid., p. 96.
5. Ibid., p. 96.
6. Ibid., pp. 150–51.
7. Ibid., p. 152.
8. Ibid., p. 158.
9. Ibid., p. 214.
10. Ibid., p. 47. Diary entry.
11. Ibid., pp. 58–59. Diary entry. Psalm 62:5.
12. Ibid., pp. 166–67. Excerpt from a letter to a relative.
13. Ibid., p. 178. Letter excerpt. Recipient unknown.

XXII

Catherine Ferguson, 1774 or 1779–1854

A Mother in Israel

"You must learn to see Christ in the black man," the Lord said to me. A week before, my husband and I had been robbed of a good camera, several lenses, and coins my grandmother gave me—substantial old dollars, buffalo nickels, one Indian head penny. Another tenant in the house, a friendly drug dealer who was usually around, having no regular employment, broke through a flimsy closet wall after walking in an unlocked front door to the apartment beside us. My husband heard him talking with his friends about how much our camera would fetch at the pawnshop. The police came. One took notes; the other leafed through a magazine. I wanted to tell them that I knew who robbed us, but my mouth failed to work.

I had been happy to move into an integrated neighborhood near Notre Dame, and I had liked our neighbor. He helped the Baptist pastor across the street move a coffin from the hearse into the church. But when he violated us, I was suddenly, irrationally, scared of every black man I saw. Then the word: "You must learn to see Christ in the black man." Only as I did this did my fear subside.

In New York City, there was a woman who tamed rough neighborhoods with her presence and ministry. She saw Christ in everyone, and they found Christ in her. She is one of our saints.

Catherine Ferguson was a professional baker, pioneer social worker, church school founder, and spiritual guide to many poor children and adults. She was born a slave as her mother, Katy Williams, traveled from Virginia to Brooklyn. Her owner, a Presbyterian elder she referred to as "R. B.," sold her mother when Catherine was just eight years old. Just before being taken away, her mother blessed her and gave her to God. Catherine was bereft, a motherless child.

When she was fourteen or fifteen, Catharine, also known as Katy, sought the counsel of Rev. John M. Mason, pastor of the Scotch Presbyterian Church on

Cedar Street, and emerged from his study at peace. Soon after joining this church, the same one to which Isabella Graham belonged, she stood at the back of the sanctuary on a communion Sunday, conscious of the cold stares of prejudiced parishioners. They did not want to sit by an African American at the Lord's Table. Pastor Mason rebuked them by walking down the aisle to meet her, grasping her hand, and leading her to a seat at the communion table.[1] She belonged to this congregation for the rest of her life.

Two or three years later, when Katy was sixteen or seventeen, two friends helped her obtain freedom. A year or so later she married and bore two children, but neither her children nor husband lived long.

Katy baked wedding cakes and smaller sponge and pound cakes, which she sold in New York from a long, narrow basket. Katy's customers always welcomed her warmly; her cakes always sold out. As a schoolgirl, Mrs. John Olcutt often stopped by Katy's home to visit. "I can recall her now in my mind as she started out," wrote Mrs. Olcutt, "the basket on her arm, her hands clasped before her, her peaceful countenance shining because of her loving spirit."[2] Katy was also a skilled lace cleaner.

Supporting oneself in New York City would have been challenge enough for most women. But Katy was extraordinary; she gave away every cent of profit to help others and threw herself into three ministries: social work, church school, and prayer meetings.

Over the course of her life she took forty-eight children out of almshouses and impoverished situations and looked after them herself or found families to care for them. These children would have otherwise lived on the streets, stealing food to survive.

On Sundays Catherine witnessed neglected children running through the streets. She founded an early church school by bringing these children into her home and arranging for teachers to give them religious instruction as well as a basic education. Catherine, who had memorized much of the Bible and was known for her "pious discourse," also participated in the students' spiritual formation. Around 1811 the classes were moved to the new Murray Street home of her congregation, and the pastor arranged for her to have more assistants. One of these was Isaac Ferris, a young theological student, who went on to become chancellor of New York University.[3]

A Mother in Israel

Annual reports of the New York Female Union Society for the Promotion of Sunday Schools, to which Catherine's school belonged, state that between 1818 and 1825, attendance averaged forty to fifty students, and in 1818 her classes served blacks and whites, children and adults.[4]

Catherine had a prayer meeting at her home every Friday evening for over forty years, and during the last five years held an additional Sunday afternoon prayer meeting for neglected neighborhood children and poor adults who didn't attend church. Is it any wonder city missionaries observed that wherever Katy lived, "the whole aspect of the neighborhood was changed"?[5]

Catherine Ferguson, a poor, illiterate woman, anticipated modern foster care and poured herself out for the spiritual welfare of others. Born into bondage and bereft of her mother at a tender age, she consented to follow Christ and was transformed from victim to healer. Benson Lossing, who included her in his book of brief memoirs of eminent Americans, considered her equal to Jesus' exemplar of loving generosity: the poor widow who gave everything she had for charitable donations (*Mark 12:41–44*).[6] The abolitionist Lewis Tappan, who wrote the full-length obituary that appeared in the *New York Daily Tribune* on July 20, 1854, affirmed her to be a "mother in Israel," one in whom the love of God was made tangible in the lives of others.[7]

Like Catherine, will you join hands with your soul friends and seek nourishment at Christ's Table, that you may become loving and generous, a blessing to others?

Here is the full text of Catherine Ferguson's obituary, an inspiring testimony to the life of a saint who enriched and transformed many lives.

The Whole Neighborhood Changed
Obituary
Died, on Tuesday, 11th, intestate, at her home, No. 74 Thompson Street, Widow Catherine Ferguson, after a brief illness, aged about 75 years. The departure of this remarkable woman should be commemorated by an obituary notice worthy of such a mother in Israel, and such an active, life-long Christian philanthropist. It is hoped that a memoir will be presented to the public. Thousands in this community have heard of or known Katy Ferguson, the aged colored woman, who in more vigorous life was the celebrated cake maker for weddings and other social parties. But many who have eaten her unrivaled cake, and been edified by her sensible chat or pious discourse, may be ignorant of the eminent virtues and

extraordinary good deeds which crowned her life. It is due, therefore, to the cause of Christ, of philanthropy, and the people of color especially, that her distinguished services should be recorded. The principal facts contained in this notice were taken down from Mrs. Ferguson's own lips, March 25, 1850.

Katy was born a slave. Her mother gave birth to her on her passage from Virginia to this city [New York]. Katy Williams, for that was her name, was "owned" by R. B., who lived on Water Street, and was an elder in one of the New York City Presbyterian churches. "R. B.," said Katy, "sold my mother away, but I remember that before we were torn asunder, she knelt down, laid her hand on my head, and gave me to God." Katy never saw her mother again. Her mistress told her that if she was as good as her mother, she would do well. Katy felt keenly the loss of her mother.

The recollection of her own anguish when separated from her made her, she said, feel compassion for children. When ten years old, she told her master, R. B., that if he would give her liberty, she would serve the Lord forever. But he did not do it.

Katy was never taught to read. "My mistress," she said, "would not let me learn; and once she said to me, 'you know more now than my daughters.' " One of her mistress's sons asked Katy to teach him geography, etc. She exclaimed, "I can't." He replied, "Yes, you can; if I don't read right in the Bible, or if I don't say my catechism right, you tell quick enough."

At fourteen years of age she was converted to God. When under conviction of sin, she determined to go and see the Rev. John M. Mason, whose church she then attended. She was afraid to go, was unwilling it should be known in the family that she went, and tremblingly apprehensive that she could not get access to Dr. Mason, or that he would not pay attention to her. She, however, summoned resolution enough to go. "While I stood at the door, ringing the bell," said she, "I cannot describe my feelings, and when the door opened and Dr. Mason himself stood before me, I trembled from head to foot. If he had spoken harshly to me or had repulsed me, I should almost died of grief, and perhaps have lost my soul." But the good man did not speak harshly to her nor repulse her. Stern and apparently haughty as he was on some occasions, he possessed kind and tender feelings, as the writer well remembers. He united two qualities that are never found united except in truly great men: high intellectual power and strong emotional feelings. Without waiting for the little trembling colored girl to say anything, Dr. Mason said, "Have you come here to talk to me about your soul?"

This greatly encouraged her. She went in and disclosed to the venerable man the secrets of her heart.

When Katy was sixteen or seventeen years old, a lady in the city purchased her freedom for $200, giving her six years to reimburse her. But she afterwards agreed to allow one half of the sum for eleven months work, and the late excellent Divie Bethune raised the other hundred dollars.[8]

At eighteen she was married. She had two children but lost them both. "They are dead," said Katy, "and I have no relations now, and most of my old friends are gone."

During her life she had taken forty-eight children—twenty of them white children—some from the almshouse and others from their parents, and brought them up or kept them until she could find places for them. She expended much money on their behalf and followed them with affectionate interest with her prayers. To my inquiry, "Have you laid up any property?" She quickly replied, "How could I, when I gave away all I earned?"

When she lived at No. 52 Warren Street (the house has since been taken down), she regularly collected the children in the neighborhood, who were accustomed to run in the street on the Lord's Day, into her house, and got suitable persons to come and hear them say their catechism, etc.

The sainted Isabella Graham used to invite Katy's scholars to her house to say their catechism and receive religious instruction. This was about the time Dr. Mason's church in Murray Street was built. The doctor heard of her school and one Sunday visited it. "What are you about here, Katy?" said he; "keeping school on the Sabbath? We must not leave you to do all this." So he spoke to his elders and had the lecture room opened and the children transferred to it. This was the origin of the Sunday school in the Murray Street church, and it is believed that Katy Ferguson's was the first Sunday school in the city.[9]

For more than forty years, up to the last of her life, she has had a prayer meeting at her house every Friday evening, and for some five years past, another every Sabbath afternoon, into which she gathered the poor neglected children of the neighborhood and those adults who did not attend church. She always secured the aid of some good man to conduct these meetings. The results of these efforts were most happy. The tract distributors, city missionaries and others remarked that where Katy lived, the whole aspect of the neighborhood was changed.

So much for the exertions of a poor colored woman who could not read! "The liberal heart deviseth liberal things."

The secret of Katy's usefulness was her fervent, uniform and consistent piety. No one could be with her even for a little while without feeling its influence. The love of God was shed abroad in her heart, and it found expression in acts of benevolence to his children. The cause of missions was very dear to her. Three years and a half ago, a company of missionaries were about to embark for West Africa under the direction of the American Missionary Association. One of the missionaries was invited to attend the little meetings held at Katy's house, and did so once or twice before leaving the country. Katy's sympathies were at once strongly enlisted in behalf of this young missionary and all his associates. A few months since, the writer met her in the street and she eagerly inquired about the Mendi mission. "These three years," said she, "I have never missed a day but I have prayed for those dear missionaries."

Katy mourned over the condition of the poor people in the city who were suffering on account of their vices as well as their poverty. She said, "The ruination of both white and colored people in this city is gambling. I told one of them that I would never do it—that I had rather live on bread and water."

On Tuesday morning, having been for several days somewhat indisposed, she went out to see a physician. She soon returned to her house and lay down, but grew rapidly worse. In a few hours, it became apparent that her disease was cholera, and she was sensible that the hour of dissolution was at hand. Notwithstanding the suddenness of the summons, she was ready. Her mind was calm and clear. "O!" said she to a friend who stood near, "what a good thing it is to have a hope in Jesus!" Her last words were, "All is well." Yes, sainted spirit, "all *is* well."[10]

A Mother in Israel

Reflection Questions

Katy's mother knelt down, laid her hand on her daughter's head, and blessed her. Do you give others tangible signs of love?

Catherine did not begin to feel at home in her congregation until the pastor took her by the hand to the communion table. Consider Hebrews 13:2: "Do not neglect to show hospitality to strangers, for by doing that some have entertained angels without knowing it." Pray to become more hospitable to others in every area of life. Is your *intent* toward others welcoming? Many people can sense whether it is.

Catherine was unable to read yet helped many children to learn. Consider Jesus' affirmation: ". . . for God all things are possible" (*Matt. 19:26*). Pray for God to use you however and wherever God wishes. Sing or read the African American spiritual "I'm Gonna Live So God Can Use Me" (*The Presbyterian Hymnal: Hymns, Psalms, and Spiritual Songs* [Louisville, Ky.: Westminster/John Knox Press, 1990], no. 369.)

Notes

1. Mrs. John W. Olcutt, "Recollections of Katy Ferguson," *Southern Workman* 52 (September 1923), p. 463.
2. Ibid., p. 463.
3. Benson J. Lossing, *Our Countrymen, or Brief Memoirs of Eminent Americans* (New York: Ensign, Bridgman & Fanning, 1855), p. 405 n. 1.
4. Allen Hartvik, "Catherine Ferguson, Black Founder of a Sunday-School," *Negro History Bulletin* (December 1972): 177.
5. [Lewis Tappan] Obituary in the *New York Daily Tribune*, July 20, 1854, p. 7.
6. Lossing, *Our Countrymen*, p. 404.
7. S.v. "Ferguson, Katy," in *African American National Biography*, vol. 3 (Oxford University Press, 2008), p. 249.
8. The "lady" may have been Isabella Graham; see chapter 18. Divie Bethune was her son-in-law.
9. This assumption appears to be incorrect. See Hartvik, "Catherine Ferguson," p. 177.
10. [Lewis Tappan] Obituary, p. 7.

XXIII

Elizabeth Prentiss, 1818–1878

She Made Our Hearts Burn Within Us

Everyone has a gift, and gifts have their own seasons: spring, summer, autumn, winter. When winter lasts a long time, we may feel numb and discouraged. God sometimes allows gifts to be buried, not to kill them but to allow new development.

The spiritual guide Elizabeth Prentiss knew all about the seasons of God's gifts. "When we are not sending any branches upward, we may be sending roots downward," she affirmed. "When everything seems a failure, we are making the best kind of progress."[1] She brought spiritual light and consolation to thousands of people through her personal presence, writings, and Bible study leadership.[2]

Elizabeth was born October 26, 1818, in Portland, Maine, to Ann Shipman and Edward Payson. Her father, a well-known and beloved Congregationalist pastor, died when she was nine. Lizzy was a frail child subject to headaches but was also studious and intense. A childhood friend recalled that she knew a lot about the Bible and was interested in her spiritual welfare. When eight years old, she convened prayer meetings that met at odd hours in odd places. During a year of school in Ipswich, New York, twelve-year-old Lizzy joined the Bleecker Street Presbyterian Church.

When she was twenty, Elizabeth, who had the gift of inspiring students, began to teach both regular and religious classes in Portland and later Richmond, Virginia. She also began to write for publication and found early success with children's stories.

By 1843 she had moved back to Portland and become engaged to George Lewis Prentiss, then a Congregational pastor. They married in April 1845 and moved to the whaling community of New Bedford, Massachusetts, where they had two children. Elizabeth began to minister to the sick and the bereaved. Her husband noted that in comforting bereaved mothers, she "seemed like one specially anointed of the Lord for [that] office."[3]

In 1850 George was called to the Second Presbyterian Church, Newark, New Jersey, and the following spring accepted the pastorate of the Mercer Street Presbyterian Church, New York. Elizabeth's health became fragile again and she began to suffer insomnia, an affliction that would plague her for many years. She bore two more children but lost them. The second pregnancy left her with what may have been an abscess near her hip joint. A nurse kept the child in a separate room, and when the child, Bessie, died, Elizabeth had scarcely held her at all.

Late in 1853 she recovered her health to some extent and resumed writing. Her book *The Flower of the Family* was published and translated into French and German.

In 1857 her husband resigned from the pastorate because of ill health, and his doctor advised living abroad for a few years. With financial support from generous parishioners they spent time in Switzerland and France, returning to New York in September 1860. Elizabeth and George had two more children who survived infancy.

As her husband entered a new pastorate amid difficulties and worry caused by the Civil War, Elizabeth endured almost continuous ill health. Her insomnia became entrenched, and caring for her younger children further undermined her strength. By 1864 she suffered from neuralgia. The assassination of President Lincoln in April 1865 hit her very hard. Desperate for relief, she went for a "water cure" and found overall improvement and some relief from her insomnia.[4]

In the next years Elizabeth continued to write. Her religious novel, *Stepping Heavenward*, published in 1869, sold 100,000 copies in the United States alone; English, French, and German editions followed. The couple bought a summer home in Dorset, Vermont, to which they repaired every summer for ten years. Overall, Elizabeth was busy and happy. In 1870 she wrote to George, "I must tell you what a busy day I had yesterday, being chaplain, marketer, mother, author, and consoler from early morning till nine at night." She recalled visiting a friend and her children and confessed that she "kept her and the girls screaming with laughter for an hour, which did me lots of good, and I hope did not hurt them."[5]

She loved to garden and could not walk outdoors without bringing home a wildflower or toadstool, a bit of moss, a bird's nest, or a leaf. She was, said a friend, a "true decorative artist," whose rooms were "bowers of beauty." She learned to paint in oil and watercolor, hobbies that gave her much pleasure. "As far as earthly blessings go," she wrote in 1873, "I am as near perfect happiness as a human being can be; everything is heaped on me."[6]

Elizabeth continued her role of spiritual guide, for which had shown a vocation as a girl. She led a meeting for Bible study and prayer in Dorset for years and led a similar group in New York for at least four years. We can catch a glimpse of her as a teacher from one who overheard a portion of her address to a large group of young women at the Collegiate Reformed Church:

"I was impressed, from so much as I did hear of her remarks, with her ability to combine rarest beauty and highest spirituality of thought with the utmost simplicity of language and plainest illustrations. Her conversation was like the mystic ladder which was set up on the earth, and the top of it reached to heaven."[7]

Over the years, Elizabeth spent many hours visiting with and consoling the sick, the dying, and the bereaved. Furthermore, she was, noted her husband, "one of God's own ministering spirits" for friends overcome by weakness, trouble, or sorrow. She also wrote many spiritual letters, always more eager "that souls should grow than that pain should cease." George affirmed her skill and discernment:

"Few have the gift or the courage to deal faithfully yet lovingly with an erring soul, but she did not shrink back from even this service to those she loved. I can bear witness to the wisdom, penetration, skill, and fidelity with which she probed a terribly wounded spirit . . . ."[8]

On August 5, 1878, Elizabeth and her two daughters took a long walk in the woods then worked on the lawn and among her flowers until she was overcome by the heat. Having been weak and nauseated for several days, she retired to bed. On August 8, still a bit weak, she drove to her weekly Bible reading in the afternoon. During the next several days she finished a watercolor picture, tended her flowers, and collected some woodland plants for her brookside garden with her husband, who presented her with a sprig of flowering clematis at the end of the afternoon. After several days of decline, she died August 13.

The center of Elizabeth's spirituality was personal holiness and communion with God. Devout from her youth, she sought to deepen her understanding through spiritual reading. Among the books she read were *The Life and Character of Miss*

Trusted Voices

Susanna Anthony, The Imitation of Christ, Bunyan's *Pilgrim's Progress,* Baxter's *Saints' Everlasting Rest,* the spiritual letters of Madame Guyon, and the work of Archbishop François Fénelon (1651–1715), which influenced her significantly. "Reserve to yourself some time to be alone with God," counseled Fénelon. "Remain there in the simplest, the freest, and the most familiar intercourse. Make of all things matter for conversation with [God]; speak to Him of all according to your heart's depths and consult Him upon everything. Silence your desires, your tastes, your aversions, your prejudices, your habits. And in this silence of your whole self, listen to Him Who is the Word and the Truth: *Audiam quid loquatur in me Dominus—'I will hear what the Lord will speak in me.'*"9 Taking the French priest for her spiritual mentor, Elizabeth made God her friend.

In 1871 Elizabeth entered a period of spiritual aridity, unable to sense God's presence. This trial strengthened and deepened her faith, and, rather than paralyzing her, catalyzed her ministry to troubled people through personal contacts and letters. By the end of 1873 her trial was over, and her faith was deeper and more fruitful. She had been so transformed that "nobody could come near her without being straightway reminded of [Christ]." Her prayer, George reflected, "was answered in the experience of many souls, whose faith was kindled into a brighter flame by the intense ardor of hers." Her utterances, wrote author Marion Harland, "made our hearts burn within us as she talked with us by the way."10

One pastor praised Elizabeth Prentiss as "one whom God commissioned, so far as we can judge, to bring light and comfort to multitudes and whom he prepared for that blessed work by peculiar and severe discipline."11 May we be so attentive to God's voice in the depth of our hearts that we may persevere in perfecting the gifts given us, even as Elizabeth endured pain, trial, and bereavement to become a soul blazing with love.

The following excerpts are from a few of Elizabeth's letters of spiritual guidance. Learn from her how to grow stronger in faith, why it is important to rest in the presence of Christ, and what grounds Christians have for peace in the midst of life's frustrations.

Look to Christ

"I dare not answer your letter, just received, in my own strength, but must pray over it long. It is a great thing to learn how far our doubts and despondencies are the direct result of physical causes, and another great thing it is, when we cannot trace any such connection, to bear patiently and quietly what God *permits,* if He does not authorise. I have no more doubt that you love Him, and that He loves you, than that I love Him and that He loves me. You have been daily in my prayers. Temptations and conflict are inseparable from the Christian life; no strange thing has happened to you. Let me comfort you with the assurance that you will be taught more and more by God's Spirit how to resist; and that true strength and holy manhood will spring up from this painful soil.

"Try to take heart; there is more than one footprint on the sands of time to prove that 'some forlorn and shipwrecked brother' has traversed them before you, and come off conqueror through the Beloved. *Don't stop praying for your life.* Be as cold and emotionless as you please; God will accept your naked faith, when it has no glow or warmth in it; and in His own time the loving, glad heart will come back to you. . . .

"You ask if I 'ever feel that religion is a sham'? No, never. I *know* it is a reality. If you ask if I am ever staggered by the inconsistencies of professing Christians, I say yes, I am often made heartsick by them; but heartsickness always makes me run to Christ, and one good look at Him pacifies me. This is in fact my panacea for every ill . . . . God purposely sickens us of man and of self, that we may learn to 'look long at Jesus.' . . . We say, 'Man's chief end is to glorify God and enjoy Him forever.' Now, can we enjoy Him till we do glorify Him? Can we enjoy Him while living for ourselves, while indulging in sin, while prayerless and cold and dead? Does not God directly seek our highest happiness when He strips us of vainglory and self-love, embitters the poisonous draught of mere human felicity, and makes us fall down before Him lost in the sense of His beauty and desirableness? The connection between glorifying and enjoying Him is, to my mind, perfect. . . . He who has let self go and lives only for the honor of God, is the free, the happy man. . . . I entreat you to turn your eyes away from self, from man, and look to Christ."[12]

Only God Can Satisfy

" 'Only God can satisfy . . . and yet we try, every now and then, to see if we can't find somebody else worth leaning on. *We never shall,* and it is a great pity we cannot always realise it. I never deliberately make this attempt now, but am still liable to fall into temptation. I am *sure* that I can never be really happy and at rest out of or far from Christ, nor do I want to be. Getting new and warm friends is all very well, but I emerge from this snare into a deepening conviction that I must learn to say, 'None but Christ.' . . . Now, dear —, it is a dreadful thing to be cold towards our best Friend; a calamity if it comes upon us through Satan; a sin and folly if it is the result of any fault or omission of our own. There is but one refuge from it, and that is in just going to Him and telling Him all about it. We cannot force ourselves to love Him, but we can ask Him to give us the love, and sooner or later He *will*. He may seem not to hear, the answer may come gradually and imperceptibly, but it will come. He has given you one friend at least who prays for your spiritual advance every day. I hope you pray thus for me. Friendship that does not do that is not worth the name."[13]

The Current Bears Us Home

"You speak in your letter of being oppressed by the heat, and wearied by visitors, and say that prayer is little more than uttering the name of Jesus. I have asked myself a great many times this summer how much that means. 'All I can utter sometimes is Thy name!'[14] This line expresses my state for a good while. Of course getting out of one house into another and coming up here, all in the space of one month, was a great tax on time and strength, and all my regular habits had to be broken up. Then before the [hydraulic] ram was put in I over-exerted myself, unconsciously, carrying too heavy pails of water to my flower beds, and so broke down. For some hours the end looked very near, but I do not know whether it was stupidity or faith that made me so content to go. I am afraid that a good deal of what passes for the one is really the other. Fortunately for us, our faith does not entitle us to heaven any more than our stupidity shuts us out of it; when we get there it will be through Him who loved us. But if I may judge by the experience of this little illness, our hearts are not so tied to or in love with the world as we fear. We make the most of it as long as we must stay in it; but the under current bears *home*."[15]

Turning Toward the Sun

"God never places us in any position in which we cannot grow. We may fancy that He does. We may fear we are so impeded by fretting, petty cares that we are gaining nothing; but when we are not sending any branches upward, we may be sending roots downward. Perhaps in the time of our humiliation, when everything seems a failure, we are making the best kind of progress. God delights to try our faith by the conditions in which He places us.

"A plant set in the shade shows where its heart is by turning toward the sun, even when unable to reach it. We have so much to distract us in this world that we do not realise how truly and deeply, if not always warmly and consciously, we love Christ. But I believe that this love is the strongest principle in every regenerate soul. It may slumber for a time, it may falter, it may freeze nearly to death; but sooner or later it will declare itself as the ruling passion.

"You should regard all your discontent with yourself as negative devotion, for that it really is. Madame Guyon said boldly, but truly, 'O mon Dieu, plutôt pécheur que superbe' ['O my God, I'd rather sin than be proud'], and that is the consoling word I feel like sending you today. I know all about these little domestic foxes that spoil the vines, and sympathise with you in yours. But if some other trial would serve God's purpose, He would substitute it."[16]

Reflection Questions

For generations Reformed people, like other Christians, have used spiritual reading as a means to become closer to God. Elizabeth was no exception.
Do you read books that lead you further into the mystery and love of God?

What purpose does Elizabeth see when God sickens us of other people and ourselves? Reflect on Elizabeth's observation "God never places us in any position in which we cannot grow." Think of a trial you have endured. How did this serve God's loving purpose?

Take heart from Elizabeth's words "We do not realise how truly and deeply, if not always warmly and consciously, we love Christ."

Trusted Voices

Notes

1. Elizabeth Prentiss, *The Life and Letters of Elizabeth Prentiss* [edited by George L. Prentiss] (New York, 1882), p. 420.
2. S.v. "Prentiss, Elizabeth Payson," in *American National Biography*, vol. 17 (New York: Oxford University Press, 1999), pp. 830–31; s.v. "Prentiss, Elizabeth Payson," *Notable American Women 1607–1950*, vol. 3 (Cambridge, Mass.: Belknap Press, 1971), pp. 95–96. I refer to the subject simply as Elizabeth Prentiss, since the surname Payson was used to link her with her famous father.
3. Prentiss, *Life*, p. 96.
4. This Victorian health trend was also called "hydropathy." Georgiana Bruce Kirby (1818–1887) writes that hydropathy was developed by a Silesian peasant named Priensnitz, who was able to cure people of various diseases. Kirby, feeling run-down by too much work and study, took a water cure under the care of a German physician, Dr. Robert Wesselhöft. The first step was to sit in a shower house while ice-cold spring water poured onto the patient's back from a height of twenty feet. "It gave the sensation of being pounded by glass balls," she wrote, "and excited the belief that no matter what insidious disease was settled in or near your spinal column, these balls would certainly dislodge it (p. 165). The regimen also called for "taking the pack," wrapped up in a wet sheet, then four or five blankets. After profuse sweating, patients were plunged into a bathtub filled with cold water, then given a breakfast of brown bread, baked apples, mush and cream, or similar food. Later in the day they walked seven to ten miles, occasionally took a sitz bath, drank numerous glasses of water, and, when tired, lay down on the ground in the sun, "tranquilized by the peaceful scenery and the song of birds." Georgiana Bruce Kirby, *Years of Experience: An Autobiographical Narrative* (New York: G. P. Putnam's Sons, 1887), pp. 161–66.
5. Prentiss, *Life*, pp. 345 n. 1; 337.
6. Ibid., pp. 358, 406.
7. Ibid., p. 448.
8. Ibid., p. 360.
9. François Fénelon, *The Spiritual Letters*, vol. 2 (London, 1893), p. 472. See Psalm 85:8.
10. Prentiss, *Life*, p. 436. "Elizabeth Prentiss," by Marion Harland, in *Our Famous Women* (Hartford, Conn., 1888), p. 557.
11. Prentiss, *Life*, p. 560.
12. Ibid., pp. 310–12. Excerpts from letter to a young friend, August 8, 1870.
13. Ibid., pp. 404–05. Excerpt from letter to a young friend, August 15, 1873.
14. Dr. L. H. Hemenway, apparently a family friend.
15. Prentiss, *Life*, pp. 410–11. Excerpt, letter to a friend, July 27, 1873.
16. Ibid., p. 420. To a Christian friend, November 12, 1873.

Epilogue

When I was a child, I found God outdoors and at church. At college I pursued a religion major; but Scripture, theology, and world religion courses did not address my inner unrest. "Are you personal or impersonal?" I asked God, and sensed that I would find an answer. One Sunday after worship, God's call came to me like lightning. "I want you to minister to people," the Voice said. I talked with Nevin Danner, a campus minister. "Why me?" Surely God did not intend that message for this shy, studious, self-centered person. But I did not yet know what God can do through people who surrender themselves to divine love.

One night at a seminary coffeehouse, God enfolded me within an overwhelming white light: loving, warm, intimate, at the same time in high contrast with myself. As the light disappeared, I bent my head in sobs.

Some months later, I was studying at the library when I was startled by a sense of the night sky opening up and the words "Are you ready to die?" I felt God's breath on my back and fled to the home of a faculty couple who welcomed me overnight. If something big was going to happen, Phil Anderson was the person I trusted to be there. I read through the letters of Paul. The night resumed its normal proportions and I went to sleep. Later I would realize that this experience was an invitation to die to self and submit to the power of Christ through the Holy Spirit—a renewal of baptism.

I could not understand what was happening to me until I stumbled across the writing of St. John of the Cross.[1] I had entered a dark night, an arduous journey to which God calls some souls.

I could not pray for many years. All I could do was surrender myself to God, endure and wait. Finally, prayer returned. I pray a lot now, especially for others.

Trusted Voices

The old creature in me still has life and so I pray "your will, not mine" and "let me be a leaf in your stream,"[2] a movement of continual surrender to God until I awake in God's likeness. I trust God. I'm not alone.

During these years, certain writers were my trusted voices: *Abandonment to Divine Providence* by Jean-Pierre de Caussade and *The Cloud of Unknowing* (anonymous author), through which I learned (again) of a simple method of prayer.[3] Yet I could not sink into the writings. I needed female voices. Not a different message, different messengers.

While working on another project, I discovered some of the women portrayed in this book. Sarah Davy (chapter 4) wrote a prayer asking the Savior to "take up thy rest here in my poor naked soul."[4] This intrigued me and I was hungry for more women's voices. The women portrayed here have been my spiritual companions for a decade. I feel more complete in their company; the childhood void is filled.

An experience of the saints in light taught me they wish to be remembered and heard (see *Heb. 12:1*).[5] They want to encourage you on your journey. Mary Simpson, Catharine Dimmick, Marion Laird, Isabella Graham, Katy Ferguson, and the others point beyond themselves. Each directs you to God, to love and serve others. Each says, "God, with whom we wrestled, whom we love and serve (even now), dwells in you, even if Love seems remote. Perhaps when you ache for God and are full of doubt, you are closer to God than you know." How do you respond?

Marion Laird looked at her heart and pronounced it a "hole of serpents." I have faced my own pit of vipers: memories of failures brought to mind repeatedly until I acknowledged my faults and sought forgiveness. Over many years I have been reshaped by unseen parental hands, the old self dying, a new creation emerging, and a painful purification.

Today, I look out the window of my first home. A tall pine tree anchors the back yard. Squirrels and chipmunks scamper under the wood fence and eat food I leave for them. A squirrel finds a child's green apple reject and gnaws at it, chunks cascading from its mouth. Chipmunks chirp like birds and share my tomatoes. The neighborhood rabbit eats grass and rests. Outside the fenced yard dogs give chase: I've seen the rabbit outrun a Labrador retriever. Sparrows have a nest in the ivy near my bedroom window. At night the insect percussion band plays.

Epilogue

In 2007, my husband of almost twenty years died following major surgery. I live alone now with two cats and a blue parrotlet, my winged cheerleader, and am at peace. I am home.

Will you trust the voice of God in Scripture and the still voice of silence to guide you? Will you cast off excuses of busyness, illness, poverty, ineptitude, or disinterest? God is intent on you. God washes through your soul with waves of warmth, love, kindness, and challenge. You cannot know just how much you can do for God until you lift your face to meet that unseen gaze and become at ease in God's presence.

If this seems too much just now, remember: trusted voices of Scripture and ancestors tell you who you are—child of God, a vessel for the Spirit, God's dwelling place, the friend of Christ. Allow these women to speak to you; and through them, hear the comfort, the strengthening voice, of our Savior: Let me share the yoke of your burden. You are not alone. You never were alone. "I am with you always" (*Matt. 28:20*).

> God most merciful,
> you are the shelter of all who seek your face,
> the strength of all who call out your name.
> You anchor me and set me free.
> You invite me to trust you with an open heart,
> that I may respond when you call.
> Look into my heart and purify me
> until your image shines clearly within,
> that I, waking to my true nature,
> may rejoice in you, love and serve you all my days;
> through Christ my Savior, in the power of your Holy Spirit.
> Amen.

Notes

1. "The Dark Night of the Soul" in *The Collected Works of St. John of the Cross*, trans. by Kieran Kavanaugh and Otilio Rodriguez, introductions by Kieran Kavanaugh (Washington, D.C.: ICS Publications, 1973), pp. 295–389. Barbara Dent's *My Only Friend Is Darkness: Living the Night of Faith* (Notre Dame, Ind.: Ave Maria Press, 1988) is more accessible and is, in part, an interpretation of St. John's writing. The title refers to Psalm 88:18 (Roman Catholic Ps. 87, Confraternity Version).
2. Source of this phrase not recalled.
3. *Abandonment to Divine Providence*, newly trans. with intro. by John Beevers (Garden City, N.Y.: Image Books, 1975); *The Cloud of Unknowing*, trans. with intro. by Clifton Wolters (Harmondsworth, Middlesex, England: Penguin Books, 1961). My introduction to contemplative prayer occurred in a spirituality group at the campus ministry center in Bloomington, Indiana, in the early 1970s.
4. Diane Karay Tripp, ed., *Prayers from the Reformed Tradition: In the Company of a Great Cloud of Witnesses* (Louisville: Witherspoon Press, 2001), p. 172.
5. Ibid., p. 1.

Acknowledgments

Divine love guided my research and writing. *Deo gratias.* I would like to thank Nancy Kahaian, Tom Schwanda, and Marcia Smith-Wood for their suggestions. The microtext librarians at the Hesburgh Library, University of Notre Dame— Shelly Bates, Barbara Connelly, Paula McDonald, and Becky Price—provided expert help with a good measure of warmth. Thank you! I am also grateful to Danielle Joyner, who retrieved material for me from limited-access sources.

Finally, I am indebted to those who approved this project and all who worked on its production. Mark Hinds, I appreciate your expertise, calm approach, and affirmation of my work. You can have my "Deadlines amuse me" placard.

Praise for Trusted Voices

"Diane Karay Tripp opens the door here to a previously little known world of writing by faith-filled women in the Reformed tradition. This book is poised to prompt thoughtful theological and spiritual reflections through its judicious excerpts of historic texts and thought-provoking discussion questions. It demonstrates the value of efforts to mine the rich historical resources of the Reformed tradition for contemporary wisdom and inspiration."

John D. Witvliet
Director, Calvin Institute of Christian Worship
Professor of Music and Worship,
Calvin College and Calvin Theological Seminary

"Who are the historic women in the Reformed tradition who can serve as saints and role models for Christians today? Diane Karay Tripp has searched high and low to collect hidden stories of women from varied backgrounds from the seventeenth through the nineteenth century who loved God well and who through their mystical experiences, service to others, or teaching still show the way. Their courage, their perseverance in the face of illness, slavery, or hardship amaze and their unstinting effort to devote themselves wholly to the love of God and humanity move and inspire. Read, ponder, and be challenged to respond more fully to God's love."

Ruth Duck
Professor of Worship, Garrett-Evangelical Theological Seminary

Praise for Trusted Voices

"In accordance with the wisdom of the writer of the Book of Proverbs that 'a woman who fears the Lord is to be praised' (31:30b), Diane Karay Tripp introduces us in this volume to praiseworthy women, whose previously silent voices are to be trusted by virtue of their authentic Christian witness. Karay Tripp's own faith-full voice presents these diverse women of the Reformed tradition, and guides the reader in appropriating spiritual insights gleaned from their life-testimonies and writings. This is a book that will speak to both the mind and the heart."

(Rev. Dr.) Karen B. Westerfield Tucker
Professor of Worship, Boston University School of Theology

"Our contemporary age is in great need of reliable and trustworthy guides. This critical necessity is heightened for women who typically are under-represented in the record of history. Therefore, women and men alike will greatly benefit from Diane Karay Tripp's wise gathering, astute biographical introductions, and inviting selections of primary sources from these Reformed female heroes. An added benefit of this rich anthology of stories of faith and devotion is that among this broad based collection of pilgrims one finds numerous Native Americans and African American representatives. Further, I was delighted to discover that Diane had included many women who had profound mystical experiences of God or served as spiritual directors to women and men. *Trusted Voices* is a valuable addition to the literature on Reformed piety and I highly recommend it. May it encourage many readers to appropriate these or seek out other contemporary trusted voices as models for faith and Christian maturity."

(Rev. Dr.) Tom Schwanda
Associate Professor of Christian Formation and Ministry, Wheaton College
Adjunct Associate Professor of Christian Spirituality,
Fuller Theological Seminary